GURUPATH

THE WHISPERING CLASSROOM

DR SHWETA N PANCHOLI

ink Scribe

Gurupath

Publisher: Inkscribe Publishing Pvt. Ltd.

ISBN Number: 978-93-344-4587-9

Guru Path: The Whispering Classroom

By Dr. Shweta Pancholi

As an educator, researcher, and emotional-learning advocate from Gujarat, India. With a strong academic background in English and teacher education, she has dedicated her career to exploring how emotional awareness, cultural sensitivity, and compassionate teaching can transform learning experiences for children—especially those from marginalized communities.

Her work reflects a blend of ancient Indian wisdom, modern emotional psychology, and holistic pedagogy. She writes with clarity and heart, drawing from years of teaching, training, mentoring, and classroom observation. Dr. Pancholi believes that education is not merely an academic process but a healing and humanizing journey. Her voice resonates with teachers, parents, and educators who wish to bring meaning and mindfulness into their practice.

This book is an extension of her vision—**to bring soul back into education, one teacher and one child at a time.**

Preface

Education has always been more than instruction. It is a quiet shaping of the human heart. It is the invisible thread that guides a child toward confidence, curiosity, and compassion. And yet, in the noise of syllabus completion and academic pressure, the soul of education often fades into the background.

This book was born from the desire to restore that soul.

Every chapter is an invitation to look at teaching with fresh, sensitive eyes—not as a job, but as a journey of understanding, healing, and connection. It is a reminder that children do not learn from subjects; they learn from people. They learn from the teacher's tone, mood, presence, and inner stability. They learn from classrooms that honour their emotions and celebrate their individuality.

Drawing from psychology, ancient Indian wisdom, modern pedagogy, personal insight, and lived experience, this book brings together the emotional truths of learning. It is a call to teachers to see themselves not just as educators, but as guides, nurturers, and transformers of lives.

May these pages bring you clarity, courage, and compassion. May they remind you that teaching is sacred work. May they honour the teacher in you—the one who touches lives silently, beautifully, and forever.

Acknowledgement

Every book carries the fingerprints of many hearts, and this one is no different.

To the children who inspired every word—your innocence, questions, fears, laughter, and resilience shaped the soul of this book. You are the reason this work exists.

To the teachers who wake up every morning and choose patience over frustration, empathy over judgment, effort over exhaustion—this book is a tribute to your unseen labour, your silent sacrifices, and your unwavering belief in children.

To the parents who trust schools with their most precious treasures—thank you for walking beside educators with hope, vulnerability, and love.

To my mentors, colleagues, and friends who encouraged my journey and reminded me of the meaning behind my work—your support nourished this creation.

To the divine grace and inner strength that guided me through every chapter—this book is an offering of gratitude.

And finally, to every reader holding this book—may it bring warmth to your heart and light to your path. May it remind you that education, at its core, is an act of love.

Introduction

Teaching is often described as a profession, but in truth, it is a human experience. It is the only work where the mind, heart, and soul come together in service of another being's growth. A teacher may stand in front of a class, but they teach far more through their presence than through their words.

In today's world, children are growing up in environments filled with speed, competition, digital noise, pressure, and emotional turbulence. Their needs have changed. Their behaviours have changed. Their dreams and fears have changed. But one thing remains constant—their need for emotionally grounded adults.

This book explores teaching from a new lens:

a lens that sees the child, understands the heart, respects the pace of growth, and values emotional safety as much as academic progress.

Across these chapters, you will journey through:

- the inner world of the child
- the emotional responsibilities of the teacher
- the importance of connection, storytelling, play, mindfulness, and culture

- the wisdom behind holistic, brain-compatible, and humane learning
- the teacher's own inner evolution

More than techniques, this book offers *understanding*.

More than information, it offers *insight*.

More than strategies, it offers *soul*.

This is a book for teachers who want to teach with heart.

For parents who wish to understand their children more deeply.

For educators seeking meaning beyond methods.

And for anyone who believes that learning should be a joyful, healing experience.

Welcome to a journey of transformation—of children, classrooms, and the teacher within.

Dedication

To every teacher who carries the light of knowledge with humility.

To every learner whose curiosity inspires the world to evolve.

To every soul who understands that education is not a profession—but a sacred path where minds awaken and hearts blossom.

Preface

Teaching is not merely an act of delivering lessons—it is a sacred interaction between consciousness and curiosity. Over the years, while working with children, teachers, and academic leaders, I realized that true education is never confined to textbooks. It lives in the warmth of connection, the strength of values, the beauty of local culture, the harmony of mind–body balance, and the inner awakening of both teacher and learner.

Guru Path – New Edition is a refined, expanded, and re-envisioned version of my earlier work. It is powered by India's ancient wisdom, infused with modern pedagogical research, and guided by the National Education Policy 2020. This book integrates psychology, Ayurveda, neuroscience, and classroom practice into one holistic framework that speaks to the teacher's head, heart, and soul.

I offer this book as a companion for educators who seek depth, meaning, and transformation in their teaching journey.

Contents

Section I

The Heart of a Guru

Chapter 1

The Calling of a Teacher: Teaching as a Sacred Sadhana

Teaching is more than a profession—it is a spiritual discipline. A teacher shapes not just minds but the very vibration of the classroom. In ancient India, the guru's work was considered tapasya: a committed effort towards uplifting another soul.

Modern classrooms may look different, but the essence remains the same. Children still seek belonging, inspiration, and stability. A good teacher informs; a great teacher transforms. When teaching becomes sadhana, the classroom becomes a shared space of growth where both teacher and learner evolve together.

A teacher's true success lies not in completing the syllabus, but in touching a life.

CHAPTER 1

THE CALLING OF A TEACHER: TEACHING AS A SACRED SADHANA

Teaching has always been more than a profession. It is an ancient responsibility carried by thousands of years of Indian wisdom. In the Vedic worldview, a teacher was not hired—he or she was *invited* into the life of a learner, just as one invites a sacred presence into a home. The guru's role was not limited to academics; it extended into shaping character, guiding emotions, nurturing discipline, and awakening the inner light of the child.

Today, classrooms may be filled with technology, decorated walls, syllabus charts, and digital tools—but the essence remains unchanged:

The teacher is still the soul of the learning experience.

Modern research supports what our ancestors already knew: a child learns best from a teacher who is emotionally stable, spiritually aware, and deeply connected with their learners. Teaching is not simply transmitting information; it is *transforming* the learner's understanding of themselves and the world.

Teaching as Sadhana

Sadhana means disciplined spiritual practice. It requires intention, dedication, patience, and purity of purpose. When teaching becomes sadhana:

- Lessons become offerings.
- Classrooms become sanctuaries.
- Students become seekers.
- The teacher becomes a guide, not an instructor.

A teacher on the path of sadhana does not ask, "How much syllabus is left?"

They ask, "How much joy have my children experienced today? How much confidence did they take back home?"

Such teachers transform learning from a burden into a celebration.

The Inner Preparation of a Teacher

Before entering a classroom, a true teacher prepares internally. This involves:

1. Clearing the Mind

A calm teacher creates calm students.

A distracted teacher creates chaos.

A moment of silence before entering the classroom can shift the entire learning environment.

2. Setting Intentions

An intention such as:

"May I guide my students with love and clarity today,"

shapes behaviour unconsciously.

3. Practising Emotional Awareness

Children absorb a teacher's emotions faster than the lesson.

A teacher who is mindful of:

- tone
- reactions
- expressions
- words

creates an emotionally safe space where learning flows naturally.

Teaching as an Act of Compassion

Compassion in teaching means more than kindness. It means understanding circumstances behind behaviour.

A child who is:

- inattentive may be overwhelmed
- angry may be hurt
- silent may be scared
- hyperactive may need movement
- rebellious may feel unseen

When teachers respond to behaviour with compassion instead of criticism, transformation begins.

A compassionate teacher empowers a child to see their worth.

The Teacher as a Mirror

Children see themselves through the eyes of their teachers.

A teacher's words become internal scripts that stay forever.

- "You are capable" – builds courage
- "I trust you" – builds responsibility
- "You made a mistake, but it's okay" – builds resilience
- "You matter" – builds identity

Even a single sentence can change the way a child views themselves.

A teacher becomes a mirror that reflects not only what a child *is*, but what they *can become*.

Teaching as Transformation, Not Transaction

In today's world, teaching is often reduced to:

- completing portions
- covering chapters
- preparing for tests
- meeting deadlines
- fulfilling administrative duties

But true teaching rises above these limitations.

Transformation happens when:

- curiosity is sparked
- confidence is strengthened
- creativity is encouraged

- values are modelled
- the heart is touched

A teacher may forget the lessons they taught,

but children never forget how the teacher made them feel.

The Legacy of a Teacher

Teachers create ripples that travel across generations.

A child inspired today becomes:

- an ethical leader
- a compassionate parent
- a responsible citizen
- a thoughtful human being

The teacher's legacy is not measured by annual results, but by lifelong impact.

No other profession shapes the inner world of another human so intimately.

Teaching as a Lifelong Journey

The world changes, and so must teachers.

Teaching is a profession that demands:

- Learning
- Unlearning
- Relearning
- Adapting

- Reflecting
- Evolving

A teacher who stops learning stops inspiring.

Teaching becomes powerful when the teacher remains a student of life.

Conclusion

Teaching as sadhana elevates the profession into a spiritual path. It transforms:

- the teacher
- the child
- the classroom
- the community
- the future

A teacher is not defined by the subject they teach, but by the lives they touch.

A teacher does not simply open textbooks—**they open minds and awaken souls.**

Chapter 2

The Guru–Shishya Bond: Beyond Curriculum

The Guru–Shishya relationship is one of the most beautiful expressions of human connection. It is grounded in trust, respect, and mutual growth. In this bond, learning becomes effortless because it flows through love, not fear.

A guru does not impose knowledge; a guru awakens it. A shishya does not merely memorize; a shishya absorbs and transforms.

When this bond is strong, the classroom becomes an ecosystem of joy.

CHAPTER 2

THE GURU–SHISHYA BOND: A RELATIONSHIP BEYOND CURRICULUM

The relationship between a teacher and a learner is the spiritual heartbeat of education. Across civilizations, cultures, and centuries, the teacher–student bond has remained one of the most transformative human relationships. It is a connection that transcends time, extends beyond the classroom, and influences the deepest layers of identity, behaviour, and purpose.

In the Indian tradition, this bond was sacred. The *guru* was not merely an instructor of subjects, and the *shishya* was not merely a receiver of information. Their relationship was one of shared evolution—a journey where both grow, both reflect, and both rise.

Today, education may have become more structured and system-driven, yet the essence of this ancient relationship remains unaltered. A powerful teacher–student bond can uplift even an ordinary classroom into a space of magic and meaning.

The Spiritual Foundation of the Guru–Shishya Relationship

The word *guru* is derived from:

- **Gu** – darkness or ignorance
- **Ru** – remover or dispeller

Thus, a guru is one who dispels darkness—not with force, but with light.

A guru:

- awakens clarity
- nurtures wisdom
- ignites purpose
- strengthens identity
- shapes character

A shishya is one who:

- trusts
- receives
- questions
- reflects
- transforms

This relationship is not based on hierarchy. It is based on mutual respect, pure intention, and inner alignment.

More Than Academics: The Layers of the Guru–Shishya Bond

The guru–shishya bond operates on multiple levels:

1. Intellectual Level

The teacher introduces concepts, knowledge, and skills.

2. Emotional Level

The teacher offers safety, belonging, acceptance, and encouragement.

3. Behavioural Level

The teacher models discipline, respect, and responsibility.

4. Cultural Level

The teacher passes values, traditions, heritage, and identity.

5. Spiritual Level

The teacher awakens consciousness, purpose, and inner strength.

A teacher who touches all five levels becomes unforgettable.

Trust: The First Foundation

A child learns best from someone they trust.

Trust grows when:

- the teacher listens
- the teacher keeps their word
- the teacher is fair
- the teacher shows consistency
- the teacher does not shame or insult
- the teacher protects confidentiality

In an atmosphere of trust, children feel safe to:

- ask questions
- make mistakes
- express emotions
- try new things

- challenge norms
- grow beyond their limits

Trust is the bridge through which real learning travels.

Respect: The Soul of the Relationship

Respect in teaching is not demanded—it is earned.

Children respect teachers who:

- speak kindly
- correct without humiliating
- are well-prepared
- practice fairness
- maintain patience
- show confidence without ego

When a teacher respects students, students naturally respect the teacher.

Respect is mutual; it is the foundation of lifelong influence.

Love: The Unspoken Language

Children thrive in the presence of love.

This love is not sentimental; it is compassionate, patient, and unconditional.

A teacher expresses love through:

- gentle tone
- encouraging words
- patient explanations

- non-judgmental acceptance
- belief in the child's potential

Love is not a weakness; it is the greatest teaching strength.

The Guru's Responsibility

The guru carries immense responsibility. The way a teacher speaks, behaves, reacts, and responds becomes a model for the learner.

A guru must:

- be self-aware
- continue learning
- keep biases aside
- protect the dignity of the child
- uplift rather than break
- inspire rather than impose
- correct without crushing confidence

A guru does not create fear.

A guru creates awakening.

The Shishya's Responsibility

The student too has responsibilities in this sacred bond. A shishya must:

- come with sincerity
- remain curious
- ask questions

- practice humility
- reflect regularly
- apply knowledge
- respect the guru's guidance

This mutual responsibility strengthens the bond into a lifelong relationship.

Communication: The Nectar of Connection

The quality of interaction shapes the quality of relationship.

A guru communicates:

- clearly
- calmly
- kindly
- confidently
- with presence

But communication is not only about speaking—it is about *listening*.

Listening to:

- what the child says
- what the child avoids
- what the child expresses emotionally
- what the child struggles with
- what the child dreams of

The guru's listening helps the shishya discover their voice.

The Modern Classroom & the Ancient Relationship

Today's learning environment is different:

- large classes
- pressure for results
- digital distractions
- diverse learning needs
- limited time

Yet the ancient guru–shishya wisdom fits beautifully even today.

A teacher can still:

- build trust
- maintain warmth
- show fairness
- understand individual needs
- support emotions
- inspire curiosity

Technology may evolve, but human connection remains timeless.

The Transformative Power of Being Seen

One of the deepest human longings is the desire to be seen—not just physically, but truly, emotionally, and spiritually.

When a teacher *sees* a child:

- their confidence rises
- their behaviour improves

- their learning becomes joyful
- their identity strengthens

A child who feels seen becomes a child who believes in themselves.

Discipline That Builds, Not Breaks

The guru–shishya bond is strengthened by discipline, but not the kind based on fear.

True discipline is:

- firm but gentle
- consistent, not erratic
- rooted in respect
- guided by purpose
- explained, not imposed

A child will follow rules when they trust the teacher's intention.

The Invisible Influence

The deepest impact a teacher makes is often invisible.

Children learn through:

- observation
- imitation
- energy
- values

- tone
- responses

A teacher's character silently shapes a child's worldview.

You teach more through who you *are* than what you *say*.

The Guru–Shishya Bond Beyond the Classroom

Some relationships end when the bell rings.

The guru–shishya bond does not.

A student carries:

- your words
- your values
- your lessons
- your mannerisms
- your encouragement
- your belief in them

into their entire life.

Years later, it is never the mark sheet they remember— it is the teacher who believed in them when no one else did.

The Gift of Lifelong Guidance

The beauty of this relationship is that it often transforms into lifelong mentorship.

Many adults still:

- consult their teachers
- remember their advice
- follow their values
- honour their influence
- shape their careers inspired by them
- name their successes after them

A guru's influence does not end with school.

It continues into adulthood, parenthood, and society.

Conclusion

The guru–shishya bond is the soul of education.

It is a relationship built on:

- trust
- respect
- love
- mutual responsibility
- communication
- presence
- compassion
- shared growth

It shapes destinies, builds character, and awakens potential.

A curriculum may instruct.

A teacher may inform.

But only a **guru** can transform.

When a teacher becomes a guru and a student becomes a shishya, learning becomes a sacred journey—not of textbooks, but of souls.

Chapter 3

Awakening the Teacher Within

Every good teacher must first be a good learner. Awakening the teacher within means embracing:

- **Self-awareness**
- **Reflection**
- **Courage to evolve**
- **Curiosity**
- **Inner discipline**

A teacher who continues to grow inevitably inspires students to grow.

CHAPTER 3

AWAKENING THE TEACHER WITHIN

Teaching begins long before a teacher steps into a classroom. It begins in the quiet spaces of the heart where intention meets purpose, where personal experiences transform into wisdom, and where one discovers a calling that is much deeper than a choice of career. Every teacher carries within them a reservoir of knowledge, compassion, intuition, and lived experiences that shape the way they connect with children. Awakening the teacher within means tapping into this inner reservoir, understanding oneself as deeply as one seeks to understand one's students, and becoming aware of the authentic self that guides every action inside the learning space.

To awaken the teacher within, one must first recognise that teaching is not an external performance—it is an internal alignment. It is the merging of who you are with what you teach. A teacher who has awakened their inner clarity stands before students not as a transmitter of information, but as a beam of light that shows the path forward. Children may learn subjects from any resource, but what they learn from an awakened teacher is something no textbook can offer: a sense of direction, a sense of belonging, and a sense of meaning.

An awakened teacher possesses an inner stillness. They are able to pause before reacting, think before judging, and understand before correcting. This composure does not come naturally—it is cultivated through reflection, self-awareness, and continuous learning. Every day in the classroom presents new questions, new challenges, and new emotional landscapes to navigate. A teacher who takes time to reflect on their own responses, thoughts, and feelings gradually awakens the inner guide who knows how to respond with wisdom rather than impulse.

Awakening the teacher within also requires reconnecting with the original spark that brought one into this profession. Every teacher begins with an ideal—sometimes it is the memory of a favourite teacher, sometimes a love for learning, sometimes a desire to make a difference. With time, administrative pressure, personal responsibilities, and societal expectations often blur that original spark. The journey of awakening is, in essence, the journey of remembering. It is the act of returning to the core belief that teaching is a sacred privilege, and that to influence a young mind is to influence the future.

A teacher is not awakened merely by attending workshops or receiving degrees. Those can enrich professional competence, but awakening comes from inner shifts—shifts in how one sees the child, how one sees oneself, and how one sees the role of education in shaping human lives. It is a deep inner understanding that every child who enters the classroom comes with a unique story, a unique temperament, a unique rhythm of learning, and a unique emotional world. Awakening the teacher within means developing the sensitivity to read these unspoken stories without needing words.

An awakened teacher pays attention not only to the content being taught, but to the emotions that flow beneath the surface. They understand that a child who appears distracted may not be careless; they may be carrying a worry from home. A child who appears restless is not disobedient; they may simply need a different learning style. A child who appears silent is not incapable; they may just need time to find their voice.

Awakening comes when a teacher sees beyond behaviour and seeks to understand the soul behind it.

This awakening is also about knowing one's own emotional patterns. A teacher who understands their triggers prevents anger from overshadowing empathy. A teacher who recognises their own anxieties does not transfer those anxieties to children. A teacher who understands their own impatience learns to cultivate patience. In many ways, teaching is a mirror; the more deeply we understand ourselves, the more deeply we can understand our students.

To awaken the teacher within is to embrace continuous learning—not out of obligation, but out of curiosity and humility. It is to acknowledge that education is not static; it evolves with society, technology, culture, and human consciousness. An awakened teacher reads not only books, but also people, experiences, and emotions. They observe the world with openness, listen without judgment, and remain willing to unlearn and relearn.

Another dimension of awakening lies in rediscovering joy—the joy of teaching, the joy of connecting, the joy of seeing even the smallest spark of understanding in a child's eyes. When teaching becomes mechanical, joy disappears. When teaching becomes human, joy returns. This joy is not dramatic or loud; it is often subtle—a moment of laughter in the classroom, a child finally understanding a concept, a shy student raising their hand, or a child offering a genuine smile of gratitude. These small moments accumulate, nourish the spirit, and keep the inner teacher awake.

Awakening also means recognising the power one holds—not power over children, but power over their own future.

A single sentence spoken by a teacher can stay in a child's memory for life. A single act of fairness can restore a child's faith in themselves. A single gesture of kindness can heal a child's hidden wound. Awareness of this influence keeps a teacher grounded and conscious of their words, actions, and energy.

The awakened teacher does not seek perfection—they seek presence. They understand that mistakes will happen, frustrations will arise, and not every lesson will go as planned. Yet even in these imperfect moments, an awakened teacher remains compassionate towards themselves. They do not carry guilt or self-blame; they carry learning forward. Their humility becomes their strength, and their resilience becomes their guide.

Ultimately, awakening the teacher within is a lifelong process. It unfolds slowly, through conscious choices, reflective thinking, and heartfelt intention. It grows through every interaction with students, every challenge faced, every insight gained. It is a journey without a final destination—because every day offers a new opportunity to grow, to listen, to understand, and to teach with greater depth and authenticity.

When a teacher awakens from within, the classroom transforms effortlessly. It becomes a space of warmth rather than fear, curiosity rather than pressure, collaboration rather than authority. The teacher becomes not just an educator, but a mentor, a guide, a gentle force shaping the emotional, intellectual, and spiritual landscape of every child they meet.

An awakened teacher does not just impart lessons—they inspire lives.

And that is the true essence of the Guru Path.

Chapter 4

The Art of Presence

Children remember teachers who were *present* with them. Presence is the power to listen deeply, observe without judgment, and respond with empathy.

A present teacher notices:

- The child who is sad but smiling
- The child who wants to speak but withdraws
- The child who learns differently
- The child who needs only one word of encouragement

Presence turns teaching into a human art.

CHAPTER 4

THE ART OF PRESENCE: CREATING SAFE EMOTIONAL SPACES

A classroom is not defined by its walls, its furniture, or its resources. It is defined by the presence of the person who stands before the students every day. Presence is one of the most powerful qualities a teacher can possess, yet it is rarely spoken about in teacher training programmes. It is not a skill one acquires through textbooks or workshops—it is an inner cultivation, a subtle blending of awareness, sensitivity, focus, and emotional intelligence. When a teacher is truly present, the classroom becomes a place of connection, safety, and trust.

Presence is the ability to give oneself wholly to the moment. It means that the teacher is not merely standing in front of the class, performing a routine, but is genuinely *there*, mentally, emotionally, and energetically. A present teacher listens not only to the words spoken by students but to the pauses, the hesitations, the silences, and even the unexpressed fears hidden in their eyes. Presence goes beyond hearing answers; it means perceiving the child's inner world.

Children intuitively know when a teacher is present. They sense it not through logic, but through emotion. A present teacher radiates calmness, confidence, and care. Their energy reassures the child that they are safe. In such a space, a child dares to raise their hand even when unsure of the answer, dares to ask questions without fear of being judged, dares to express themselves even if their voice trembles. Presence breaks the invisible barriers between teacher and student, creating a human connection where learning becomes a joyous experience instead of a pressure-driven task.

However, the art of presence is not easy to cultivate in the modern world. Teachers often find themselves consumed by administrative duties, syllabus deadlines, large class sizes, and personal responsibilities that drain emotional energy. Yet presence is not about having a perfect environment; it is about creating a moment of attentiveness despite the noise around. Even in a chaotic classroom, a teacher who pauses, breathes, and centres themselves regains the power to ground the room.

When the teacher is present, discipline becomes less about authority and more about influence. Students feel guided, not controlled. They behave better not out of fear, but out of respect. Presence neutralises the need for harsh reprimands or repeated instructions, because children respond naturally to the steady energy of an attentive adult. A teacher's presence acts like the still centre of a moving storm—anchoring, calming, and balancing everything around.

Presence also plays a significant role in identifying the emotional needs of students. A teacher who is present notices when a usually cheerful child is quiet, when a confident child is unusually withdrawn, when a diligent child seems distracted, when a restless child is unusually subdued. These changes often signal emotional turbulence, familial difficulties, academic pressure, or internal struggles that may not be verbalised. A present teacher becomes a subtle emotional guide, offering support, reassurance, or simply a listening ear to the child who needs it.

Creating safe emotional spaces begins with non-judgment. A present teacher does not interpret every misbehaviour as disrespect, nor every silence as disinterest. They understand that children navigate complex feelings they may not know how to articulate. Instead of reacting impulsively, they respond with patience and understanding. Presence allows the teacher to ask, "What is this child trying to communicate through this behaviour?" This simple shift—from reacting to understanding—transforms the entire classroom atmosphere.

One of the greatest gifts a teacher can give students is the feeling that they are seen—truly seen. When a teacher acknowledges a child's efforts, remembers their interests, appreciates their strengths, or simply calls them by their name with warmth, the child experiences validation. Presence makes every child feel valued. Even the most introverted or academically struggling student blossoms when they sense that the teacher notices their existence, contributions, and potential.

Presence also has a profound impact on learning. Neuroscience shows that the brain learns best in an environment of safety and trust. A present teacher creates such an environment, allowing students to focus deeply, absorb information more effectively, and retain knowledge longer. When the teacher's mind is scattered or anxious, children mirror that energy and exhibit similar restlessness. Conversely, when the teacher is composed and centred, it brings steadiness into the classroom. The teacher's state becomes the emotional climate of the room.

Cultivating presence requires conscious practice. It begins with slowing down the mind, even for a few seconds before entering the class. A deep breath, a moment of grounding, or a silent intention can shift the teacher's entire energy. During lessons, presence means giving attention to one task at a time—listening when students speak, observing when they work, guiding when they struggle. It means being aware of one's tone, facial expressions, and body language, because these silently shape the learning environment.

Presence also requires teachers to acknowledge their own emotions. A teacher who denies their stress, frustration, or fatigue cannot maintain consistent presence. Instead, an aware teacher accepts these feelings, understands them, and prevents them from spilling onto children. Emotional honesty with oneself is the root of emotional stability with others.

Creating a safe emotional space also involves vulnerability. A teacher who occasionally shares their own experiences, mistakes, or challenges becomes relatable. Students feel comforted knowing that growth is a shared journey, not a performance. Presence does not make the teacher rigid; it makes them human.

Ultimately, the art of presence transforms the classroom from a space of instruction to a space of connection. Children flourish where they feel emotionally safe. They take risks, ask questions, explore freely, and engage deeply. The teacher becomes the anchor of this emotional ecosystem—steady, compassionate, mindful, and aware.

Presence cannot be taught through techniques alone; it must arise from the teacher's inner quietness and intention. It blossoms when the teacher understands that their role is not limited to teaching lessons but to nurturing lives. A present teacher does not merely complete the syllabus—they create memories, build confidence, and leave impressions that last far beyond school years.

When a teacher is truly present, learning becomes human. And when learning becomes human, education becomes powerful.

Here is your **FULLY ELABORATED, NARRATIVE-STYLE CHAPTER 5**, written just like a professionally published education book. No bullet points. No listing. Smooth, rich, emotional–academic balance.

Chapter 5

The Neuroscience of Compassion

Modern neuroscience proves what ancient teachers always knew: A compassionate teacher rewires the learner's brain for safety, curiosity, and growth.

Compassion:

- Reduces classroom stress
- Improves attention
- Builds trust
- Enhances motivation
- Supports emotional regulation

A gentle voice can do what strict discipline cannot.

CHAPTER 5

TEACHING WITH COMPASSION: THE NEUROSCIENCE OF EMPATHY

Compassion has always been at the heart of the teaching profession, but only in recent years has science begun to explain why it is such a powerful force in learning. Long before neuroscientists studied brain chemistry, ancient gurus understood that knowledge blooms in the presence of kindness and withers in the presence of fear. Today, modern research validates this wisdom: a compassionate teacher literally changes the brain of the child sitting before them.

Empathy and compassion are not soft additions to education—they are the psychological and neurological foundations that determine how deeply a child can learn, how safely a child can express themselves, and how confidently a child can grow. A teacher's tone, their choice of words, their facial expressions, and even their silent presence send signals to a child's brain, shaping their emotional state and cognitive abilities.

When a teacher speaks with warmth or listens with patience, the child's brain releases oxytocin—a hormone that reduces stress and increases trust. A calm teacher lowers the child's cortisol levels, allowing the brain's learning centres to open. Conversely, harshness, humiliation, or unpredictability activate the child's amygdala—the fear centre—shutting down creativity, reasoning, and memory. This explains why children may fail to perform in a threatening environment but excel when they feel emotionally safe.

A compassionate teacher is therefore not simply being "nice"—they are creating the neurological conditions necessary for learning to occur.

Compassion begins with understanding that every child walks into the classroom carrying an invisible world. Some come with the weight of family conflicts, academic pressure, social anxiety, or emotional wounds. Others carry dreams, fears, questions, and unspoken hopes. Compassion allows the teacher to see beyond behaviour and into the emotional truth behind it. A child who disrupts the class may be seeking attention because they feel unseen. A child who argues may be masking insecurity. A child who avoids eye contact may be battling shame or self-doubt. Compassion transforms the teacher's gaze; instead of asking, "What is wrong with this child?" the compassionate teacher asks, "What has this child experienced, and what does this child need?"

Compassion in teaching is not synonymous with indulgence. It does not mean lowering standards or excusing harmful behaviour. Instead, it means responding from understanding rather than reaction. A compassionate teacher sets boundaries firmly but gently. They correct behaviour without attacking identity. They discipline without damaging dignity. They guide the child with fairness, not anger.

A compassionate classroom becomes a healing space. Children who have experienced judgment or neglect elsewhere find solace in the teacher's presence. For many children, school is the only place they encounter consistent kindness. A simple smile, a patient explanation, or a soft acknowledgement like "I understand you're upset" may be the emotional nourishment that child has been waiting for.

The neuroscience of compassion teaches us that emotions are contagious. A calm teacher calms the class. A frustrated teacher spreads frustration. Children mirror the teacher's emotional patterns, not because they choose to, but because their brains are wired for connection. This is why the teacher's emotional regulation becomes a model for students. When a teacher breathes deeply before responding, the child learns to do the same. When a teacher expresses empathy, children learn empathy. When a teacher shows patience, the classroom breathes patience.

Compassion also builds resilience in children. When a child is supported emotionally, their brain strengthens neural pathways related to self-regulation, problem-solving, and confidence. They learn to face challenges without melting into fear. They develop a stronger sense of "I can." Compassion plants seeds of inner strength that may blossom years later in adulthood.

Furthermore, compassion enhances academic outcomes. Children who feel safe participate more, ask more questions, and show greater persistence in solving difficult tasks. They take intellectual risks without fear of failure. Their curiosity flourishes because they know that mistakes will not lead to humiliation. A compassionate teacher does not simply teach lessons—they build an emotional foundation that allows the child to explore knowledge bravely.

Compassion also softens collisions that naturally occur in learning. There will always be moments when a child forgets homework, reacts impulsively, or struggles to understand a concept. The difference lies in how the teacher responds. A reaction rooted in frustration closes the child. A response rooted in compassion opens the child. When a teacher says, "Let's try again together," the child's brain shifts from defensive mode to learning mode.

Another dimension of compassionate teaching lies in acknowledging the teacher's own humanity. A compassionate teacher extends kindness not only to students but also to themselves. They recognise that perfection is unattainable, and they treat their own mistakes with the same understanding they offer their learners. When teachers practise self-compassion, they free themselves from the inner burden of guilt, allowing them to remain emotionally present for their students.

Compassion becomes a way of being when the teacher embodies certain attitudes: curiosity, patience, humility, and a willingness to understand before being understood. A teacher who practices compassion realises that behind every behaviour there is a story; behind every struggle there is an unmet need; behind every silence there is a message waiting to be heard.

In the classroom, compassion illuminates the unseen. It is the soft glance toward the child sitting alone. It is the gentle encouragement given to the child afraid to speak. It is the patience shown to the child who learns slowly. It is the warmth shared with the child who comes from a broken home. Every compassionate act, no matter how small, adds to the emotional architecture of the child's life.

Ultimately, compassion is the silent curriculum that runs beneath every lesson. It shapes character more deeply than words can. A compassionate teacher does not merely teach students—they touch the essence of who the students are becoming. Long after lessons fade, formulas are forgotten, and textbooks gather dust, the compassion of a teacher remains alive in the memory and behaviour of the child. It becomes part of their emotional DNA.

When teaching is infused with compassion, education transforms. It becomes not an obligation, but a relationship. Not a performance, but a connection. Not an instruction, but an awakening.

A compassionate teacher does not just teach the brain—they reach the heart.

And once the heart is reached, the mind follows willingly.

Section II

Understanding the Learner

Chapter 6

Child Psychology Through the Indian Lens

Indian education has always viewed the child as *poorna*—complete.

Every child brings unique prakriti, temperament, creativity, and learning rhythm.

Understanding a learner means understanding:

- Home culture
- Emotional climate
- Developmental stage
- Social environment
- Inner world

A teacher who understands the child teaches the soul, not just the brain.

CHAPTER 6

CHILD PSYCHOLOGY THROUGH THE INDIAN LENS

Understanding a child is one of the most profound responsibilities of a teacher. Yet, modern education often tries to understand children only through models borrowed from the West—Freud, Piaget, Vygotsky, Erikson, Skinner. While these frameworks have value, they do not fully capture the emotional, cultural, and spiritual richness of the Indian child. India's ancient wisdom has always approached childhood through a holistic lens, seeing the child not just as a developing cognitive mind but as a complete being—*sharir, manas, buddhi, and atma*—body, mind, intellect, and soul.

In Indian philosophy, a child is considered *poorna*—complete—not empty or unfinished. The role of the teacher is not to "fill" the child, but to help unfold what is already present within. This approach shifts the focus from control to guidance, from instruction to nurture, from pressure to presence. The Indian lens views childhood as a phase of sacred unfolding, where individuality and divinity co-exist beautifully.

An Indian child grows up in a blended environment of tradition, family systems, diverse languages, cultural practices, festivals, rituals, values, and spiritual stories. This environment profoundly shapes their psychological development. A teacher who understands this layered context can connect more deeply with the student, speak to their inner world, and guide them with sensitivity.

The Indian child's psyche is built not only through personal experiences but also through the collective consciousness of the family. Unlike in many Western cultures, where independence is emphasised early, Indian families cultivate bonds, interdependence, emotional closeness, and shared responsibility. The child often absorbs the emotions of the entire household—the stress of parents, the authority of elders, the warmth of grandparents, and the expectations of society. Their identity is not an individual shape; it is a collection of many emotional imprints.

This interconnected upbringing makes Indian children emotionally intuitive. They can sense moods, tensions, or unspoken expectations at home. They learn early to adjust, observe, decode, and respond. For this reason, Indian children often do not express their distress openly. Their silence carries meaning. Their smile may hide anxiety. Their obedience may mask fear. Their mischief may be a cry for attention. A sensitive teacher, therefore, must learn to read what is not said.

The Indian lens also emphasises that every child is born with a unique prakriti—an innate nature shaped by a blend of temperament, energies, and tendencies. Ayurveda explains this through the three doshas—Vata, Pitta, and Kapha—which shape not only physical constitution but also psychological patterns. Some children are naturally imaginative and quick-moving. Others are focused and confident. Some are gentle, calm, and grounded. Understanding these temperamental differences helps a teacher move away from the idea that there is only one "right" way for children to learn or behave.

Psychology through the Indian lens also recognises the deep role of imagination in development. Indian childhoods are filled with stories of gods, heroes, folk tales, festivals, and moral narratives. These stories do more than entertain—they shape values, emotional intelligence, creativity, and moral reasoning. A child exposed to mythological stories learns courage, sacrifice, justice, love, humility, and devotion long before they learn these concepts academically. Their psychological development is rooted in rhythm, symbolism, and narrative—a powerful tool for emotional learning.

Another essential aspect of Indian child psychology is the balance between discipline and freedom. Indian parenting often combines love with boundaries, guidance with flexibility. Children are taught respect for elders, yet encouraged to explore creativity. They learn responsibility early, yet are allowed the innocence of childhood. This duality shapes a psyche that is adaptable, resilient, and emotionally rich—but also sensitive to harshness or humiliation.

This sensitivity is crucial to understand. Because Indian children are raised in emotionally connected environments, they respond more deeply to tone and relationship than to rules or rewards. A stern word from a teacher can hurt them more than a punishment. A kind gesture from a teacher can motivate them more than a prize. The Indian child learns best not from fear, but from relationship.

Understanding child psychology also means recognising the impact of academic pressure. Indian society places immense value on education as a means of security and respect. This expectation often weighs heavily on children. Many internalise the belief that marks define their worth. Teachers who understand this internal struggle can help balance ambition with emotional well-being, teaching children that success is not measured by a report card but by personal growth.

Spirituality plays an equally important role in the Indian child's psychology. Even without formal teaching, children absorb spiritual concepts early—through prayers, traditions, rituals, and cultural practices. This spiritual grounding gives Indian children a natural inclination towards reflection, gratitude, connection, and inner awareness. When teachers integrate mindfulness, stillness, values, and ethical discussions into the classroom, they align with this existing psychological foundation.

The Indian lens also sees childhood as an era of innocence and divinity. Children are believed to be closest to their purest selves in this phase. Their laughter, curiosity, and spontaneity are seen as signs of inner purity. When teachers honour this purity, they create an environment where children's natural strengths can flourish. When teachers suppress it with criticism, comparison, or excessive control, the child's inner spark dim.

To understand a child in the Indian context is to understand their layered identity—cultural, emotional, spiritual, social, and familial. It is to recognise that their behaviour is the outcome of many influences working together. A teacher who adopts this holistic understanding becomes more patient, more empathetic, and more attuned.

Child psychology is not merely a subject to be studied—it is a lens to see children with compassion, depth, and cultural insight. When teachers adopt the Indian approach—seeing the child as a whole being rather than a collection of academic tasks—they create classrooms where children feel understood, valued, and seen.

Such classrooms become spaces where children do not simply learn—they grow. They do not merely listen—they engage. They do not merely perform—they blossom.

When we understand the child through the Indian lens, we honour not just the learner, but the soul within the learner.

And in doing so, we honour the true purpose of education.

Chapter 7

Ayurveda & Learning: Vata, Pitta, Kapha Minds

Ayurveda identifies three primary learning dispositions:

Vata Child (Creative & Sensitive)

Learns through movement, stories, rhythm.

Pitta Child (Focused & Driven)

Learns through logic, challenges, leadership tasks.

Kapha Child (Grounded & Patient)

Learns through repetition, routine, stability.

When teaching methods match prakriti, learning becomes natural.

CHAPTER 7

AYURVEDA & LEARNING: UNDERSTANDING VATA, PITTA, AND KAPHA MINDS

Ayurveda, the ancient Indian science of life, is often spoken of in the context of health, diet, and healing. Yet, at its heart, Ayurveda is a profound science of human nature. It offers the deepest insights into why people think differently, learn differently, respond differently, and grow differently. When applied to education, Ayurveda becomes a powerful psychological framework—helping teachers see learners not as uniform minds, but as unique inner worlds shaped by their *prakriti*, their natural constitution.

Every child is born with a dominant combination of three energies—Vata, Pitta, and Kapha. These are not merely physical traits; they are emotional patterns, behavioural rhythms, cognitive tendencies, and learning preferences. They guide the way a child processes information, expresses emotions, forms relationships, and responds to challenges. Understanding these subtle differences does not limit children; it liberates them. It helps teachers create learning experiences that resonate with each child's natural way of being.

In most classrooms, teachers encounter children who seem restless and imaginative, children who seem confident and focused, and children who appear calm and steady. These differences are not random—they are the expressions of the three Ayurvedic doshas. When teachers understand the doshic nature of the mind, they no longer ask, "Why is this child like this?" Instead, they begin to ask, "How can I teach this child in the way their mind understands best?"

The Vata Learner: The Wind of Imagination

A child dominated by Vata energy carries the qualities of wind—movement, lightness, speed, and creativity. Their imagination is boundless, their curiosity endless, and their thoughts flow faster than words can capture. They learn best through experiences that involve stories, visuals, play, rhythm, and novelty. Their minds dance with ideas, but this dance can sometimes look like distraction. When a Vata child forgets homework, loses things, or daydreams, it is not defiance—it is simply their mind moving rapidly in multiple directions.

Such children need warmth, reassurance, grounding routines, and gentle reminders. They flourish when given creative freedom but collapse under harsh control. They learn beautifully when the teacher engages their senses, uses metaphors, narrates examples, and creates activities that allow movement. A Vata child blooms when the classroom feels like a landscape of exploration rather than a fixed structure of discipline.

The Pitta Learner: The Fire of Focus

A Pitta child carries the qualities of fire—clarity, intelligence, ambition, and determination. Their minds are sharp and precise. They enjoy challenges, leadership roles, debates, and tasks that involve logic and structure. A Pitta learner asks questions not to test the teacher but because their mind is hungry to understand the "why" behind everything.

These children thrive when given the freedom to think critically, solve problems, and express opinions. They appreciate teachers who are clear, consistent, and fair. However, because their inner fire burns strongly, they may be quick to react when they feel misunderstood or unjustly treated. A Pitta child responds best to respect; a soft, dignified tone calms them more than strictness ever could. When their intelligence is nurtured with compassion, they grow into confident, balanced leaders.

The Kapha Learner: The Earth of Stability

A Kapha child is rooted in the qualities of earth—calmness, patience, steadiness, and emotional depth. They learn slowly but deeply. They retain concepts for longer periods and thrive in environments that feel safe, predictable, and affectionate. These children may appear quiet or shy, but their inner world is rich and observant. Once a concept clicks, they master it with grace and thoroughness.

Kapha learners respond best to warmth, encouragement, and gradual learning. They need time, not pressure. They perform exceptionally when teachers acknowledge their quiet strengths rather than comparing them to fast performers. Their steady nature is their greatest gift; they bring harmony to the classroom and possess immense resilience when nurtured properly.

Ayurveda teaches that no child is purely Vata, Pitta, or Kapha; they are unique combinations of these energies. When one dominates, it colours their learning patterns. But all three energies exist within every child, creating infinite variations of personality and intelligence. This is why Ayurveda celebrates diversity—not as a challenge, but as a natural reality.

When teachers understand the doshas, they stop trying to fit all children into one teaching style. Instead, they adapt, adjust, and respond with awareness. The restless child is no longer labelled "problematic"; the slow child is no longer "weak"; the questioning child is no longer "argumentative." Each child becomes a unique universe, deserving of a unique approach.

The beauty of applying Ayurveda in education lies in its compassion. It reminds teachers that children are not misbehaving—they are simply expressing their nature. They are not slow—they may be Kapha learners absorbing deeply. They are not inattentive—they may be Vata minds exploring creatively. They are not stubborn—they may be Pitta minds seeking clarity.

This shift in perception transforms the classroom from a place of correction into a place of understanding. It allows the teacher to guide with empathy rather than frustration. It helps the child feel seen rather than judged. And when children feel seen, they flourish.

Ayurveda also invites teachers to understand their own nature. A Vata teacher may bring creativity but struggle with structure. A Pitta teacher may bring clarity but struggle with patience. A Kapha teacher may bring warmth but struggle with assertiveness. When teachers understand themselves, they gain insight into how they teach, how they respond, and how they can grow.

Ultimately, Ayurveda is not about categorising children—it is about honouring their individuality. It teaches that education is not a mechanical process but a relationship between energies. It shows that learning becomes joyful when the teacher flows with the child's nature instead of pushing against it.

When the classroom aligns with the natural rhythms of the mind, learning feels effortless.

When the teacher understands those rhythms, teaching becomes art.

And when both align, education becomes harmony.

Chapter 8

Emotional Needs of Today's Learners

Today's children face:

- Academic pressure
- Comparison
- Social media anxiety
- Competition
- Disconnection from nature

Their deepest emotional needs are:

- Safety
- Belonging
- Expression
- Clarity
- Encouragement

A teacher who nurtures these needs becomes unforgettable.

CHAPTER 8

THE EMOTIONAL NEEDS OF TODAY'S LEARNERS

The emotional landscape of childhood is changing rapidly. Children today grow up in a world far more complex than the one their parents or teachers knew. The pace of life is faster, the pressure to perform is greater, and the sense of comparison has become constant and unavoidable. Academic expectations have intensified, family dynamics have shifted, and the influence of social media has infiltrated almost every corner of a child's inner world. In the midst of all this noise, the emotional needs of children have grown deeper, more varied, and more urgent.

Every child who walks into the classroom carries an emotional story that is often invisible to the teacher's eye. Some carry the weight of over-expectation; some carry the fear of failure; some are anxious, some lonely, some overwhelmed, and some quietly hopeful. A child may appear cheerful yet be struggling inside; another may appear restless but desperately seeking connection; another may be silent because they carry burdens too heavy for words. To teach today's learners, a teacher must see beyond the surface, tune into the emotional undercurrents, and respond with empathy rather than assumption.

The first emotional need of today's learners is *safety*—not just physical safety, but psychological safety. A child who feels judged, compared, or threatened cannot learn with an open mind. Fear closes the brain's learning centres and replaces curiosity with anxiety. In a psychologically safe environment, children feel free to ask questions, make mistakes, admit confusion, and express their opinions without fear of ridicule.

This safety is created not by rules but by the teacher's presence, tone, and mindset. When a teacher responds with patience rather than irritation, encourages rather than criticises, and listens rather than dismisses, the classroom transforms into an emotionally secure space.

Another major emotional need of today's children is *connection*. Despite the illusion of digital connectivity, many children feel emotionally disconnected. They may have hundreds of online friends but very few real relationships that offer genuine warmth and understanding. A classroom can become a place where a child feels seen, valued, and understood—if the teacher cultivates a relationship built on trust. Even a few minutes of meaningful interaction can satisfy a child's emotional hunger. A simple "How are you today?" asked with sincerity can be enough to remind them that they matter.

Children also need *clarity*. The rapid flow of information in the modern world can overwhelm them. They are exposed to academic pressure, news, social conflicts, family expectations, and peer opinions at an early age. Their minds often feel crowded, their emotions tangled. They need teachers who can help them make sense of confusion—teachers who break concepts into understandable pieces, simplify the complex, and offer clear guidance. Clarity reduces emotional distress and gives children a sense of direction.

One of the most unspoken emotional needs of today's learners is *freedom from comparison*. In earlier generations, comparison existed but was limited to close circles. Today, social media exposes children to constant comparison with thousands of peers. Achievements, looks, talents, and lifestyles are displayed and judged publicly. Many children internalise these comparisons and begin to doubt their worth. A teacher's words can either deepen this wound or heal it. When teachers celebrate individual progress rather than public competition, children begin to appreciate their own journey.

Children today also need *emotional expression*. They need safe spaces where their feelings are acknowledged rather than dismissed. A teacher who says, "It's okay to feel upset," or "I understand that you're frustrated," validates the child's emotions and teaches them to accept rather than suppress their feelings. Suppressed emotions do not vanish; they grow into stress, behavioural issues, or withdrawal. Emotional expression is not a distraction from learning—it is essential for healthy cognitive development.

Another pressing emotional need is *belonging*. More than ever, children need to feel that they are part of a community where they are accepted without conditions. Belonging creates stability. It gives children the courage to participate, explore, and believe in themselves. A teacher who fosters a sense of belonging helps prevent emotional isolation. When children feel like they are a valued part of the class, they develop confidence and empathy. A child who feels they belong behaves more responsibly because they care about their community.

Children also need *encouragement*—not empty praise, but genuine encouragement that recognises effort and growth. Today's learners often fear making mistakes because failure is magnified in a world obsessed with perfection. Encouragement allows children to embrace mistakes as part of learning. It tells them that they are not defined by their performance but by their perseverance. Encouragement builds inner strength, turning challenges into opportunities.

Today's children also need *slowness*—a break from the constant rush. Their minds are overloaded with academic work, extracurricular activities, digital distractions, and social expectations. They rarely get the space to breathe, reflect, or simply *be*. A teacher who incorporates moments of silence, mindfulness, or slow-paced learning offers children a much-needed pause. This pause helps regulate emotions, reduce stress, and improve mental clarity.

Many children today also struggle with *self-worth*. They have been conditioned to believe that their value depends on marks, appearance, popularity, or external validation. Teachers play a crucial role in reshaping this mindset. When a teacher acknowledges a child's kindness, effort, creativity, or unique qualities, the child begins to see themselves differently. They learn that their worth is intrinsic, not earned through achievement.

The emotional needs of today's children also include *stability*. Many come from homes where emotional stability is inconsistent. Family conflicts, financial pressures, or changing environments can create emotional turmoil. The teacher—through consistency, patience, and predictability—becomes the stable adult in a child's life. This stability becomes the anchor that helps the child navigate emotional storms.

Above all, children need *acceptance*. They need to feel accepted for who they are—not for who adults want them to be. Acceptance does not mean ignoring areas that need improvement; it means guiding without shaming, correcting without breaking, loving without conditions. A child who feels accepted becomes emotionally free to grow into their best self.

Understanding these emotional needs does not require special training; it requires heart. It requires slowing down, observing deeply, listening sincerely, and responding gently. The modern child needs teachers who can balance academic expectations with emotional nourishment. When children feel emotionally understood, they learn faster, behave better, and build healthier identities.

In the end, education is not only about shaping intelligent minds; it is about shaping wholesome human beings. When a teacher fulfils the emotional needs of children, they do far more than improve academic performance—they help build resilient, confident, compassionate individuals who will carry emotional health into adulthood.

A child whose emotional needs are honoured learns not merely with the mind but with the whole being.

And that is when learning becomes a lifelong gift.

Chapter 9

The Quiet, The Bold & The Restless Child

Every classroom contains diverse personalities.

A wise teacher adapts:

- The **Quiet Child** needs encouragement to speak.
- The **Bold Child** needs guidance, not suppression.
- The **Restless Child** needs movement, not punishment.

Each child has a message hidden in their behaviour.

CHAPTER 9

THE QUIET CHILD, THE BOLD CHILD, AND THE RESTLESS CHILD: UNDERSTANDING HIDDEN LANGUAGES

Every classroom is a miniature universe. Within its four walls live children with entirely different worlds inside them—worlds shaped by temperament, upbringing, fears, strengths, dreams, and experiences that the teacher may never fully know. A single lesson may be heard by thirty children, but it is experienced in thirty different ways. Some children sit silently, absorbing every word. Others sit upright, eager to speak. Some shift in their seats, unable to contain the energy that flows through them. These variations are not behavioural problems; they are expressions of individuality.

Among these varied learners, three broad patterns emerge most commonly: the Quiet Child, the Bold Child, and the Restless Child. Understanding these temperaments is not merely a behavioural exercise; it is an act of emotional interpretation. Each of these children speaks a different language. Each carries a message hidden beneath behaviour. And each needs a teacher who can read their unseen truth with compassion and insight.

The Quiet Child: The World Behind the Silence

The quiet child is often misunderstood. Their silence is mistaken for shyness, disinterest, or lack of confidence. Yet, quietness is not a deficiency; it is a temperament. Quiet children feel deeply, observe keenly, and think profoundly. They may not be the first to raise their hand, but their thoughts are often rich, imaginative, and carefully formed.

A quiet child's mind functions like a still lake—calm on the surface, but reflecting everything around it with remarkable clarity. They listen not only with their ears but with their entire being. They absorb emotions in the room, pick up unspoken tensions, and think before they speak. Their silence is not emptiness; it is fullness waiting for the right moment.

Many quiet children come from homes where reflection, politeness, or emotional restraint are valued. Others may carry social anxiety or fear of judgment. Some may be introverts by nature, finding comfort in inner worlds rather than external noise. Teachers must remember that silence is not a sign of weakness—it is simply another way of being.

To teach the quiet child, a teacher must approach gently. A harsh tone can shut them down completely. A welcoming smile can draw them out slowly. When encouraged with kindness, quiet children eventually reveal their brilliance. They may speak softly, but their insights can be powerful. They excel in activities that allow reflection—writing, drawing, observing, connecting ideas, or solving problems at their own pace.

Quiet children bloom not when pushed, but when invited.

The Bold Child: The Fire of Expression

The bold child is the one whose presence fills the room. They speak freely, question confidently, and often take initiative without hesitation. Their energy is assertive. Their personality radiates outward. But boldness is not arrogance—it is courage wrapped in enthusiasm. Bold children are often mislabeled as "attention-seeking," yet their desire to speak arises from a natural impulse to express, lead, and engage.

These children often think quickly and feel strongly. They want to participate, to contribute, to prove themselves. Boldness comes with a certain emotional fire—the child may be competitive, passionate, and driven. They may challenge ideas not out of disrespect but out of intellectual hunger. They shine when given responsibility, leadership tasks, or opportunities to present and create.

However, bold children also carry vulnerabilities beneath their confident exterior. Their outspokenness may hide insecurity. Their assertiveness may hide sensitivity. They may fear failure as deeply as the quiet child fears judgment. A bold child who is not understood may become argumentative; one who is nurtured becomes a natural leader.

Teaching the bold child requires balance—firmness without severity, encouragement without excessive praise. Bold children respond strongly to fairness. They can detect inconsistency instantly. A teacher who respects their intelligence gains their lifelong loyalty. A teacher who belittles them damages their self-esteem more deeply than one might imagine.

Bold children flourish not when controlled, but when guided.

The Restless Child: The Energy That Speaks Through Movement

The restless child is often the one who is misunderstood the most. Their body moves even when they want to sit still. Their fingers tap, their feet swing, their eyes wander. But this restlessness is not defiance; it is energy seeking expression. Their mind does not move slowly—it races ahead. Their thoughts come rapidly, and their body attempts to keep pace.

Restlessness may arise from high creativity, sensory sensitivity, or simply a temperament that thrives on movement. These children are not "badly behaved"—they are kinesthetic learners. They understand the world by touching, doing, exploring, and experiencing physically. Traditional classrooms, which demand stillness and quietness, become suffocating for them.

When a restless child is repeatedly scolded, they begin to internalise the belief that something is wrong with them. Slowly, their enthusiasm dulls. Their natural curiosity folds inward. What the teacher sees as misbehaviour is often the child's attempt to release energy that their body cannot hold.

To teach the restless child, a teacher must bring flexibility. Allowing movement-based activities, giving classroom responsibilities, using hands-on learning tools, or offering short breaks works wonders. These children respond best to positivity and structure. When given tasks that channel their energy—distributing materials, leading group activities, demonstrating concepts—their restlessness becomes productive engagement.

Restless children blossom not when punished, but when understood.

The Hidden Languages Beneath Behaviour

What makes these children truly different is not their behavior, but the *language* in which they communicate.

The quiet child speaks the language of depth.

The bold child speaks the language of expression.

The restless child speaks the language of movement.

A teacher who tries to make all children behave the same way ends up silencing natural intelligence. But a teacher who learns these hidden languages unlocks the true potential of every child.

When teachers tune into these emotional languages, they stop asking,

“What is wrong with this child?” and begin asking,

“What is this child trying to express?”

This shift transforms the classroom.

The Responsibility of the Teacher

Every child deserves to be understood on their terms. The quiet child needs encouragement, not pressure. The bold child needs respect, not suppression. The restless child needs structure, not punishment. When these needs are met, each child’s strengths rise naturally to the surface.

A quiet child grows into a thoughtful writer, researcher, or listener.

A bold child grows into a communicator, innovator, or leader.

A restless child grows into an explorer, creator, or problem-solver.

The teacher’s role is not to change who they are but to help them become the best version of themselves.

The Beauty of Diversity

A classroom filled with different temperaments is not a challenge; it is a gift. Quiet children bring calmness and reflection. Bold children bring energy and courage. Restless children bring creativity and movement. Each child completes the classroom the way different instruments complete a symphony.

When a teacher embraces these differences, the classroom becomes a world where every personality has a place, every voice matters, and every child feels seen.

A quiet child learns from the bold one.

A bold child softens through the quiet one.

A restless child balances through the grounded one.

Children do not need uniformity; they need understanding.

Conclusion

The quiet child, the bold child, and the restless child are not categories—they are windows into the infinite variety of human nature. Behaviour is merely the outer layer; beneath it lies a universe of emotions, needs, strengths, fears, and possibilities. A wise teacher looks beyond the behaviour and sees the soul.

When teachers recognize and honour these differences, they do not just manage a classroom; they nurture human beings. They become translators of silent stories, protectors of hidden dreams, and guides who help each child walk their own unique path.

A child understood becomes a child empowered.

And a child empowered becomes a future transformed.

Chapter 10

Learning Disabilities & Strength-Based Teaching

Learning disabilities are not deficiencies—they are different processing styles.

A strength-based approach focuses on:

- What the child *can* do
- How they learn best
- What motivates them
- Which environment supports them

Children learn beautifully when we stop labelling and start understanding.

CHAPTER 10

LEARNING DISABILITIES & STRENGTH-BASED TEACHING

A child's mind is a vast landscape—full of peaks of brilliance, valleys of vulnerability, pathways of curiosity, and hidden tunnels of potential waiting to be discovered. Yet, in the pressure-driven structure of modern schooling, children who think differently or learn differently are often misunderstood. Instead of asking *why* a child struggles, education systems often measure the child only by *how much* they struggle. This narrow lens gives rise to labels, judgments, and assumptions that overshadow the child's true abilities.

Learning disabilities have long carried unnecessary stigma, not because they are inherently limiting, but because society has misunderstood their nature. A learning disability does not mean a lack of intelligence. It does not mean laziness, defiance, or disinterest. It simply means that the child's brain processes information in a different way—a way that traditional systems may not always accommodate.

In reality, children with learning disabilities often possess remarkable strengths that lie outside conventional academic measurements. They may excel in creativity, problem-solving, empathy, imagination, observation, innovation, or artistic expression. The tragedy is not the disability—it is the failure to recognise the child beyond it.

Understanding learning disabilities requires a shift in perception. A child with dyslexia is not struggling because they are incapable; they are struggling because their brain processes language differently. A child with ADHD is not inattentive by choice; their mind is wired for movement and rapid thinking. A child with dysgraphia is not careless; their hand–brain coordination works differently. A child with dyscalculia is not weak in maths; they simply understand numbers in a non-linear manner. These differences are not flaws—they are neurodiverse expressions of human intelligence.

Yet, when these children enter a rigid system that expects every mind to learn identically, they encounter frustration, shame, and self-doubt. The classroom becomes a battlefield where they fight not just academic challenges but emotional wounds. Many of them internalise the belief that something is "wrong" with them. This belief remains long after school, shaping their identity in ways that take years to heal.

This is where a teacher's understanding becomes transformative. A knowledgeable and empathetic teacher can change the entire course of a child's life. By recognising the signs early, by responding with patience, and by adapting teaching methods, a teacher can turn the child's struggles into strengths. The teacher becomes the bridge between the child's inner world and the outer demands of learning.

Strength-based teaching begins with the belief that every child has abilities that must be nurtured. Instead of focusing on what the child cannot do, it asks:

What can this child do beautifully? How does this child learn naturally? What ignites this child's interest?

A strength-based approach allows the teacher to discover the child's unique way of understanding the world. Some children learn through visuals, others through movement, others through hands-on activities, and others through stories and analogies. When teaching aligns with the child's natural rhythm, learning becomes joyful instead of painful.

Consider a child who struggles to read but excels in creating vivid mental images. Such a child may thrive with picture-based learning, audiobooks, dramatizations, or storytelling. Another child who struggles with writing may express themselves beautifully through speech or creativity. A child who cannot sit still may learn mathematics faster while walking, tapping, or manipulating objects. These strategies do not "fix" disabilities; they honour diversity.

Strength-based teaching also brings emotional healing. When a teacher highlights a child's strengths—creativity, humour, kindness, imagination—the child begins to see themselves differently. Their confidence grows. Their willingness to try increases. Their fear of failure reduces. Slowly, the child learns that they are more than their challenges. A teacher's words like "You are very good at this," or "You have a special way of thinking," can become seeds of resilience that bloom throughout their life.

Children with learning disabilities also need emotional patience. Their struggles often invite frustration—not just from teachers, but from within themselves. They may compare themselves with peers, fear embarrassment, or carry guilt for disappointing adults. A patient teacher helps them feel safe. Safety is the soil in which growth happens. When a child feels accepted, their inner barriers soften, and learning begins to flow again.

Strength-based teaching also means redefining success. Success is not only the ability to spell correctly, write neatly, or calculate quickly. Success is curiosity, courage, persistence, and growth. When teachers recognise this broader understanding, they create room for every kind of intelligence to flourish.

A teacher's language plays a crucial role. Phrases like "Try again, let's work together," "I know you can learn this," "Mistakes help us grow," and "Everyone learns differently," reshape the child's emotional landscape. Words can wound, but words can also heal. A compassionate teacher uses language that uplifts rather than diminishes.

The role of the teacher extends to collaborating with parents, counsellors, and specialists. Learning disabilities need not isolate the child; they can unite a community of caring adults who understand and support the child's journey. When teachers, parents, and professionals work together, children receive a consistent message: *You are capable. You are valued. You are more than these challenges.*

Strength-based teaching does not deny the disability. It acknowledges it without letting it define the child. It creates strategies for learning while nurturing emotional confidence. It focuses on progress, not perfection. It sees the child as a whole person—mind, heart, body, and soul.

When learning disabilities are viewed through the lens of strength rather than deficit, children begin to shine. They discover abilities that were hidden behind fear. They develop confidence that can withstand challenges. They become resilient adults who know that struggle is not a limitation—it is a different path to wisdom.

In the end, the true disability lies not in the child's mind but in the system that refuses to adapt to diverse minds. A teacher who embraces strength-based teaching becomes not a corrector of weaknesses, but a celebrator of potential. They show the world that intelligence is not one-dimensional but a spectrum of infinite colours.

When a teacher sees the child beyond the disability, the child begins to see themselves beyond the disability.

And that is when true learning begins.

Section III

Pedagogy of the Soul

Chapter 11

Teaching Through Connection

Connection is stronger than control.

A connected classroom experiences:

- Fewer discipline issues
- More engagement
- Higher motivation
- Greater trust

When the teacher connects, learning flows.

CHAPTER 11

TEACHING THROUGH CONNECTION: THE HEART BEFORE THE MIND

Teaching is often described as a transfer of knowledge, a delivery of information from one mind to another. But in truth, real teaching happens long before the lesson begins. It begins the moment a teacher looks at a child with understanding, warmth, and genuine presence. It grows in the invisible space between two human beings—a space filled with trust, safety, and emotional resonance. When this space becomes alive, learning unfolds naturally. This is the power of teaching through connection.

Connection is the invisible thread that binds the teacher and the child. It is not created through rules, instructions, or authority, but through the simple, human act of relating. Children do not learn from teachers they fear, nor do they learn deeply from teachers who remain emotionally distant. They learn from teachers who care, who listen, who pause, who notice, who smile, who respect, and who communicate with authenticity. A connected teacher does not simply teach *subjects*—they teach *human beings*.

Connection begins with the recognition that children are not empty vessels waiting to be filled. They come to school with inner worlds already shaped by their homes, cultures, personalities, hopes, and challenges. A teacher who acknowledges this complexity steps into the classroom with humility rather than authority. They understand that teaching is not an act of dominance but an act of partnership.

When a child feels connected to the teacher, a new relationship emerges—one rooted in trust. Trust is the soil in which curiosity grows. It is the foundation upon which confidence is built. A child who trusts their teacher dares to ask questions, dares to experiment, dares to be wrong, and dares to try again. Even the most shy or hesitant child begins to bloom when they feel emotionally held by the teacher's presence.

Connection requires the teacher to be real. Children possess an extraordinary capacity to sense authenticity. They can tell when a teacher is genuinely interested or merely performing their role. A teacher who shows sincerity in both praise and correction earns a child's respect effortlessly. When the teacher says, "I am here with you," not through words but through tone and behaviour, the child opens up.

Connection also involves listening—not just hearing the child's words, but listening to the emotion behind them. When a child says, "I don't understand," they may be expressing confusion, fear, frustration, or even shame. When a child acts out, they may be revealing unmet emotional needs. When a child withdraws, they may be hoping for someone to notice their silence. A teacher who listens with the heart, not just the ears, becomes a bridge to the child's inner world.

In a connected classroom, mistakes become opportunities. Instead of feeling embarrassed or defensive, children feel supported. They know that the teacher will not ridicule or punish them for being imperfect. This safety allows them to take intellectual risks. A child who feels emotionally connected becomes more resilient because they know they are not alone in their struggles.

Connection transforms discipline as well. Children naturally respect teachers who respect them. They respond better to gentle reminders than to harsh scolding. When a teacher addresses misbehaviour with curiosity instead of anger—"What happened? Why did you react this way?"—the child feels understood rather than attacked. Connection does not mean permissiveness; it means guiding behaviour through relationship rather than fear.

A connected teacher uses their presence consciously. The way they enter the classroom, the way they make eye contact, the way they respond to a child's question—all create emotional signals. When the teacher approaches a child at eye level, speaks calmly, or acknowledges the child's feelings, connection becomes stronger. These tiny gestures may seem small, but they create a profound sense of belonging.

Connection also flourishes through appreciation. Children bloom when someone notices their efforts, however small. When the teacher says, "I saw how hard you tried," or "I noticed you helping your classmate," the child feels valued. Appreciation nourishes self-esteem. It teaches children that they matter beyond their academic performance.

Another vital aspect of connection is consistency. Children feel safe when the teacher's behaviour is stable and predictable. Consistency in expectations, tone, and reactions tells the child, "You can trust me." In a world where many children face instability at home or in society, the teacher becomes a pillar of emotional security. This stability is itself a connection—a silent assurance that the child can rely on the teacher's presence.

Connection also means celebrating individuality. A connected teacher does not compare children; they honour each child's unique rhythm of learning. They understand that every child has a different emotional temperament—some need gentle encouragement, others need freedom, and some need more structure. Connection grows when the teacher adapts to these differences rather than forcing uniformity.

Teaching through connection redefines success. The teacher is no longer evaluated by how many chapters they completed, but by how many hearts they touched. They measure progress not by marks alone but by confidence, curiosity, kindness, and emotional growth. They see education not as a race, but as a journey of becoming.

One of the greatest signs of a connected classroom is joy—the soft joy of learning, the quiet joy of understanding, the warm joy of being seen, and the collective joy of growing together. Joy emerges naturally when children feel emotionally safe. It makes the teacher's work lighter and makes the classroom a place children look forward to returning to.

In the deepest sense, teaching through connection is a spiritual act. It is an alignment between two souls. It is a reminder that education is not merely about shaping the future—it is about shaping the present moment with love, awareness, and humanity. When a teacher teaches through connection, they become more than an educator; they become a mentor, a guide, a nurturer, and a steady light in the child's life.

A teacher who connects with the heart leaves an imprint that lasts long after the lessons are forgotten. Long after children graduate, they remember not what the teacher taught, but how the teacher made them feel. They remember the compassion, the encouragement, the understanding, and the moments of connection that shaped their identity.

Teaching through connection is not a method—it is a way of being. It is the art of reaching the heart before reaching the mind. And when the heart opens, learning follows effortlessly.

Chapter 12

Brain-Compatible Teaching

The brain thrives on:

- Patterns
- Visuals
- Movement
- Choice
- Curiosity
- Real-life context

Teaching becomes powerful when it aligns with neuroscience.

CHAPTER 12

BRAIN-COMPATIBLE TEACHING: ALIGNING LEARNING WITH HOW THE MIND WORKS

To teach effectively, one must understand the instrument through which all learning occurs: the human brain. For centuries, teaching relied primarily on tradition, experience, and cultural expectations. While these are valuable, recent advances in neuroscience have opened a new window into understanding how children actually learn. When educators align their teaching with the natural rhythms of the brain, learning becomes not only more efficient but more joyful, meaningful, and emotionally safe.

A brain-compatible classroom does not depend on expensive resources or advanced technology. It depends on a teacher who understands that every child's brain seeks safety, connection, curiosity, and relevance. When these needs are met, learning flows like a river. When they are ignored, learning becomes a struggle.

One of the most important discoveries in neuroscience is the role of emotions in learning. The brain does not separate thinking from feeling; they are deeply intertwined. A child who is anxious, fearful, or stressed cannot learn effectively because the emotional centres of the brain dominate and shut down higher-order thinking. Conversely, when a child feels safe, appreciated, and connected, the brain releases chemicals that enhance memory, focus, and motivation. This explains why children learn better from teachers who show warmth and clarity and why harshness or humiliation can freeze their ability to process even simple information.

A brain-compatible approach also recognises that attention is not constant. A child cannot focus endlessly, nor can they absorb complex information without breaks. The brain works in cycles. It needs moments of engagement followed by moments of pause. When a teacher allows short breaks, moments of silence, or shifts in activity, they are not wasting time—they are strengthening learning. The brain needs variety to stay awake. A child who moves, reflects, talks, or plays is not distracted; they are refreshing their neural circuits.

Another insight from neuroscience is the power of relevance. The brain prioritizes information that feels meaningful or connected to real life. Children learn best when they understand *why* something matters. A lesson about plants becomes alive when connected to their garden at home. A math concept becomes meaningful when applied to shopping or daily life. A story becomes unforgettable when linked to their own experiences or emotions. The more relevant the learning, the deeper the retention.

The brain also loves patterns. It seeks structure, connections, and relationships between ideas. When a teacher explains concepts by linking old knowledge with new information, the brain forms stronger memory networks. Repetition done meaningfully strengthens these networks further. But repetition without context becomes mechanical, adding little value. Brain-compatible teaching blends structure and creativity in ways that allow students to anchor learning naturally.

Another key principle is the importance of movement. Movement stimulates the brain, increases blood flow, and enhances cognitive performance. A child who fidgets is not misbehaving; their brain is seeking stimulation. Allowing children to stand, stretch, walk, or engage in hands-on activities activates multiple areas of the brain and increases learning. A classroom where children are allowed to move is not chaotic—it is neurologically aligned.

The brain also thrives in environments of curiosity. Curiosity activates the brain's reward system, releasing dopamine, which motivates the child to explore, question, and learn more. When a teacher asks thought-provoking questions, presents puzzles, allows experiments, or uses storytelling, the child's brain becomes active and engaged. Curiosity is not a luxury—it is a biological requirement for deep learning.

The social brain is another crucial concept. Humans are wired for social interaction, and children learn significantly through observation, collaboration, and shared experiences. A brain-compatible classroom encourages group discussions, peer learning, role plays, and shared problem-solving. Children learn best when they interact—not when they sit silently for hours. Collaboration activates empathy, communication skills, and emotional bonding, making learning multi-dimensional and memorable

Safety, too, is central. The brain's threat detection system is constantly active. A single harsh comment or a moment of humiliation can send a child's brain into survival mode. In this state, learning stops. A brain-compatible teacher uses gentle correction, predictable routines, and respectful language. The goal is not to eliminate discipline but to deliver it in ways that protect the child's dignity and sense of worth.

Another remarkable insight is the role of choice. Even small choices—such as choosing a book to read, selecting a partner for group work, or deciding how to present an assignment—enhance a child's engagement. Choice activates the brain's executive functions, strengthens decision-making skills, and increases ownership of learning. A child who has a sense of control learns with greater motivation and confidence.

Brain-compatible teaching also highlights the importance of multisensory learning. The brain stores information more deeply when it has been seen, heard, touched, discussed, or created. This is why activities like drawing, building, enacting, singing, writing, and observing are powerful tools. The more senses involved in learning, the stronger the neural connections become.

Another cornerstone is feedback. The brain responds to timely, specific, and encouraging feedback. It needs to know what it did well and where it can grow. Vague praise or harsh criticism does little good. Meaningful feedback guides the brain toward improvement without triggering shame or fear. When feedback focuses on effort rather than innate ability, children internalize the belief that learning is a process, not a performance.

Finally, the brain needs hope. It needs to believe that learning is possible, growth is achievable, and mistakes are part of the journey. A hopeful learning environment nurtures resilience. A teacher's belief in the child becomes the child's belief in themselves. This belief is not abstract; it creates real changes in the brain's wiring. A child who feels hopeful becomes confident, motivated, and willing to take risks.

Brain-compatible teaching is not a set of techniques—it is a philosophy rooted in compassion, science, and respect for the natural design of the human mind. It acknowledges that learning is not mechanical but organic. It flows when the teacher understands the brain's needs and adapts their methods accordingly.

When teachers teach in harmony with the brain, learning becomes effortless. The classroom becomes alive with energy, curiosity, connection, and discovery. Children not only learn more effectively but also retain a lifelong love for learning.

In the end, the brain is not a vessel to be filled, but a garden to be nurtured.

A brain-compatible teacher becomes the gentle gardener—creating the right climate, planting seeds with care, and watching each child bloom in their own unique rhythm.

Chapter 13

The Art of Storytelling

Stories are the heartbeat of Indian learning systems.

Stories:

- Teach values
- Expand imagination
- Improve memory
- Build emotional intelligence
- Make concepts unforgettable

A teacher who tells stories, teaches twice.

CHAPTER 13

THE ART OF STORY telling: WHERE LEARNING MEETS THE SOUL

Stories are the oldest teachers in the world. Long before the existence of classrooms, textbooks, exams, and formal education systems, human beings learned through stories. Our ancestors gathered around fires, under the shade of trees, or in temple courtyards, passing down wisdom from one generation to another through narrated experiences. Storytelling was the first curriculum, the first pedagogy, the first emotional connection between the teacher and the learner.

In India, storytelling has always been woven into the fabric of life. The Ramayana was not read—it was *told.* The Mahabharata was not memorized—it was *lived* through centuries of narration. Folk tales, moral parables, mythological epics, and family stories shaped the Indian child's imagination long before printed books arrived. Through stories, children learned courage from Arjuna, loyalty from Hanuman, patience from Mahavir, compassion from Buddha, wisdom from Birbal, and resilience from countless folk heroes whose names changed across regions but whose messages remained timeless.

When stories enter the classroom, they bring with them this ancient tradition of wisdom. They awaken curiosity, open emotional doors, and create a bond between teacher and child that no textbook can replace. A story speaks not just to the mind but to the heart. It carries lessons wrapped in emotion, meaning, and wonder It transforms learning from memorization into experience.

When a teacher tells a story, something magical happens. The classroom stops being a physical space and becomes a world of imagination. Children do not merely listen—they travel. They see forests, mountains, kingdoms, oceans, and faraway lands. They meet characters who feel alive, face conflicts that mirror life, and experience emotions that help them understand their own. A classroom filled with the sound of a story becomes a living organism, breathing with excitement, curiosity, and anticipation.

Storytelling is powerful because it mirrors the way the brain learns. The human mind naturally seeks sequences, emotions, characters, and meaning. A fact may be forgotten, but a story stays. Long after a child forgets dates or formulas, they remember the story that made them laugh, cry, imagine, or think. Story-based learning activates multiple regions of the brain—memory, emotion, sensory perception, and cognitive reasoning. It becomes a whole-brain experience.

But the art of storytelling is not merely about narrating events. It is about creating connection. A teacher who tells a story becomes more human, more relatable, and more emotionally accessible. Their voice carries warmth. Their expression carries empathy. Their presence carries intention. Children feel drawn to this vulnerability and authenticity, and through it, they feel safe to express their own emotions.

Every story carries layers. On the surface, there is entertainment. Beneath that lies meaning. And beneath meaning lies transformation. When a teacher narrates a fable about honesty, a child does not feel lectured; they feel inspired. When they hear a story about perseverance, they do not feel pressured; they feel motivated. Stories allow values to enter the heart naturally, without force.

Even in academic subjects, stories are bridges. A scientific concept becomes vivid through the story of a discovery. A historical event becomes alive through the experiences of the people who lived it. A mathematical principle becomes easier when wrapped in a narrative. Children understand better when their imagination is engaged.

Stories also honour diversity. Every child sees the same story differently. The quiet child may immerse themselves in the emotions of the characters. The bold child may identify with heroes who take action. The restless child may live through the movement, conflict, and adventure within the tale. A single story touches each child in their own language of learning.

The beauty of storytelling lies in its flexibility. It can calm a restless class. It can energize a sleepy one. It can soften a tense moment. It can open a difficult topic. It can teach, heal, guide, and uplift. A teacher who masters storytelling holds a treasure chest of emotional tools.

The most powerful stories often come from the teacher's own life. When a teacher shares a personal experience—a childhood memory, a moment of struggle, a lesson learned, or an experience of kindness—children listen differently. Personal stories build trust. They reveal the teacher's humanity. They create emotional intimacy. They give children permission to share their own experiences.

Storytelling also teaches emotional intelligence. Through characters, children learn empathy by stepping into someone else's shoes. Through conflicts, they learn problem-solving.

Through resolutions, they learn hope. Through symbolism, they learn to interpret life. Stories help children understand not just the world around them but the world within them.

In a world driven by digital distraction, storytelling becomes even more essential. Stories reawaken the child's natural imagination, which screens often suppress. They bring children back to the world of deep attention, rich imagery, and emotional nuance. They remind children that real connection happens in human voices, not in pixels.

The art of storytelling also strengthens the teacher. It sharpens creativity, improves communication, deepens empathy, and brings joy into the classroom. A teacher who tells stories experiences teaching not as a task but as a celebration.

Ultimately, storytelling is not a method—it is a relationship. A story is a hand extended from the teacher's heart to the child's heart. When the story is received, the hands meet. That moment of meeting is where learning happens, silently and beautifully.

Long after the textbooks have changed, long after the curriculum has evolved, long after the school year has ended, a child remembers the stories their teacher told. Those stories stay woven into their memories, shaping their values, strengthening their courage, comforting them in difficult times, and guiding them in moments of confusion.

A story told with love becomes a story lived forever.

Chapter 14

Play, Movement & Nature

Children learn naturally when they:

- Touch
- Explore
- Observe
- Move
- Imagine
- Feel nature

Nature is the greatest classroom ever created.

CHAPTER 14

PLAY, MOVEMENT & NATURE: RETURNING CHILDHOOD TO THE CHILD

Childhood, in its purest essence, is meant to be a dance—a dance of curiosity, movement, wonder, and unrestrained joy. It is a time when the body longs to explore, the heart longs to express, and the spirit longs to discover its place in the world. Yet, in the structured world of modern education, childhood is often compressed into chairs, confined within walls, and burdened with expectations that silence its natural rhythm. Children are asked to sit still before their muscles are ready, to concentrate before their minds are steady, and to perform before their hearts feel safe.

In this silent struggle, something precious is lost—the innate relationship children have with play, movement, and nature. These three elements are not luxuries in education; they are essential nutrients for healthy development. They shape the child's physical well-being, emotional balance, cognitive growth, and spiritual connection with life itself.

Play is the language of childhood. It is how children make sense of their world. They do not play to learn; they learn because they play. When a child builds a sandcastle, they are exploring structure. When they role-play as teachers or parents, they are understanding relationships. When they run, jump, build, paint, or imagine, they are developing not only muscles and skills but also resilience, confidence, and joy. Play teaches without teaching, heals without medicine, and nurtures without instruction.

But in many modern classrooms, play is reduced to a five-minute break or a reward for finishing work. Childhood becomes a checklist, and play becomes an afterthought. A teacher who understands the true nature of learning knows that play is not the opposite of learning—it is the foundation of learning. A playful classroom awakens curiosity, strengthens attention, and invites creativity. Children feel emotionally free in the presence of play. Their minds open, their stress melts, and their natural love for learning blossoms.

Movement, too, is a fundamental part of childhood. Children are not designed to be still for long periods. Their bodies are built for exploration, and their brains thrive on physical activity. Movement stimulates neural pathways, enhances concentration, improves memory, and releases emotional tension. A child who moves is not being disruptive—they are being natural.

When a teacher allows movement in learning—through actions, dramatization, gesture-based memory techniques, hands-on work, or simple stretching—the classroom becomes alive. Children remember better when their bodies are engaged. Their attention lasts longer. Their emotions remain balanced. Movement is medicine for the restless child, confidence for the shy child, and joy for every child in-between.

Yet, one of the greatest gifts that movement offers is emotional release. A child who is anxious, frustrated, or confused may not have the words to express their feelings. But through movement, their emotions find an outlet. A brief walk, a physical activity, or a playful game can shift the emotional climate of the entire classroom.

And then there is nature—the forgotten teacher of the modern world. Nature has always been the original classroom. Long before schools existed, children learned from rivers, trees, skies, seasons, animals, and the rhythm of the earth. Nature offers lessons that no textbook can replace. It teaches patience through the growth of a seed, resilience through the bending of a tree in the wind, change through the shifting of seasons, and beauty through the colours of the sky.

Nature grounds children. It slows their racing minds, softens their anxieties, and nourishes their senses. Even a few minutes spent outdoors can refresh their emotional energy and restore calmness. In a world filled with screens and schedules, nature gives children the gift of stillness. They listen to sounds they often ignore—the rustling of leaves, the chirping of birds, the whisper of wind. These simple experiences deepen their awareness, enhance mindfulness, and bring them closer to themselves.

Nature also awakens responsibility. When children water plants, care for animals, or observe natural cycles, they develop empathy and ecological sensitivity. They begin to understand that they are a part of a larger universe—interconnected with earth, water, air, and all living beings. This awareness lays the foundation for values like respect, gratitude, and environmental stewardship.

Bringing nature into education does not require elaborate gardens or forests. It can be as simple as studying the sky from the schoolyard, caring for a small plant in the classroom, using natural materials in lessons, or taking occasional nature walks. What matters is the experience, not the scale.

Play, movement, and nature complement one another beautifully. When children play outdoors, they merge movement with nature. When they imagine games in the open air, creativity flows effortlessly. When they explore the world around them, curiosity deepens. These experiences strengthen their cognitive abilities while nurturing their emotional health.

Children who are allowed to play freely are often more self-assured.

Children who are allowed to move are often more focused.

Children who spend time in nature are often more grounded and resilient.

A teacher who embraces these elements does more than teach lessons—they protect childhood itself. They allow children to be children. They create an environment where learning feels organic, joyful, and alive. They honour the wisdom of ancient education systems, where children learned by touching, listening, observing, experimenting, and connecting with life around them.

Education does not need to be a battlefield of performance. It can be a garden. A garden where play is the sunlight, movement is the fresh air, and nature is the soil. In such a garden, every child blooms differently, beautifully, and naturally.

When schools remember the importance of play, children regain their laughter.

When they honour movement, children regain their energy.

When they reconnect with nature, children regain their soul.

And when all three return to the classroom, education becomes whole again.

Here is your **FULLY ELABORATED, CALM, SPIRITUAL, PUBLISH-READY CHAPTER 15**, written in the same rich, flowing, narrative style. No bullet points. No lists. Just a deep, immersive chapter.

Chapter 15

Mindfulness, Breath & Silence

Just one minute of silence a day can change the class.

Mindfulness:

- Enhances focus
- Reduces stress
- Improves memory
- Builds self-awareness

Silence is not absence of sound—it is presence of awareness.

CHAPTER 15

MINDFULNESS, BREATH & SILENCE: AWAKENING CALMNESS IN LEARNING

In a world filled with noise, speed, and constant stimulation, silence has become a rare luxury. Children today wake up to rushing mornings, crowded schedules, buzzing screens, and a flood of information that allows little space for stillness. Their minds remain in a perpetual state of motion—always thinking, always reacting, always processing. In such a state, learning becomes a burden rather than a joy. The mind cannot absorb deeply when it is restless, just as a lake cannot reflect the sky when its surface is disturbed.

This is where mindfulness, breath, and silence enter the realm of education—not as techniques, but as lifelines. They help the child return to themselves. They give the mind the pause it craves. They create a gentle space where attention becomes sharper, emotions become calmer, and learning becomes more meaningful.

Mindfulness is simply the art of being present. It teaches children to anchor their awareness in the here and now—not in yesterday's mistakes or tomorrow's fears. When children learn to focus on the present moment, their internal storms begin to settle. A mindful child listens better, thinks more clearly, and feels more stable within. A mindful classroom does not eliminate noise; it teaches children how to remain centred amid the noise.

The breath is the doorway to this inner calm. It is the one tool every child always carries. Breath is both physical and emotional—it reflects the state of the mind. A rushed breath reveals anxiety. A shallow breath reveals fear. A gentle breath reflects calmness. When children learn to breathe consciously, they learn to regulate their emotions. They begin to understand the subtle connection between mind and body. A single slow breath can soften irritation, reduce nervousness, and restore focus.

Introducing simple breathing practices in the classroom can create profound shifts. A minute of deep breathing before a lesson creates a sense of readiness. A pause of conscious breathing after a heated moment resets the emotional atmosphere. Breath becomes a silent teacher, reminding children that tranquility is always available within them.

Silence, the third pillar, is perhaps the most transformative. Silence is not the absence of sound; it is the presence of awareness. It is a space where the mind can rest, reset, and rejuvenate. For children who are constantly stimulated, silence becomes an anchor that grounds their wandering thoughts. When the classroom enters a moment of silence, it becomes sacred—a shared pause where every child returns to themselves.

Even thirty seconds of silence can shift the energy of the classroom. Children who were restless become calmer. Children who were distracted become attentive. Children who were overwhelmed feel their emotions soften. Silence creates an environment where learning flows naturally, without force.

Mindfulness, breath, and silence together create an emotional climate that protects the child's mental well-being. They reduce stress, enhance concentration, and strengthen self-awareness. Children who practise these regularly begin to understand their own emotions better. They learn not to react impulsively. They develop patience. Their confidence grows because they realise they can manage their internal world with grace.

These practices are not foreign to Indian culture. They are deeply rooted in our heritage. Ancient gurukulas began their learning day with a moment of silence. Rishis passed down knowledge through meditative awareness. Pranayama was not only a yogic practice but a life practice. Chanting, stillness, and mindful observation were naturally woven into learning. Modern classrooms have moved away from these roots, but the child's mind continues to crave what ancient wisdom knew well—calmness is the beginning of clarity.

Mindfulness does not require elaborate rituals. It can begin with observing the breath, listening to sounds around, paying attention to sensations, or noticing thoughts without judgment. These simple practices help children become aware of themselves, enhancing emotional intelligence. When children learn to witness their emotions, they no longer feel controlled by them.

Breath work is equally simple. A few slow inhalations and exhalations can be enough to calm a noisy class or help students transition between subjects. Breath synchronises the mind and body, creating a sense of unity within the child.

Silence, too, can be introduced gently—a silent beginning to the day, a quiet reflection after a lesson, or a moment of pause before answering questions. These small moments accumulate over time, nurturing emotional maturity.

When mindfulness, breath, and silence become part of the classroom, the teacher also transforms. Teaching becomes less stressful, less rushed, and more harmonious. The teacher's own mind becomes steady, allowing deeper connection with students. The classroom becomes a place of peace rather than pressure, a place where both teacher and learner breathe, pause, and grow together.

Children who learn to sit with their thoughts become emotionally resilient adults. They grow into individuals who respond rather than react, who pause before making decisions, who stay centred in chaos, and who carry inner peace wherever they go. This is the greatest gift education can offer—not just academic knowledge, but the inner stability required to use that knowledge wisely.

Mindfulness awakens awareness.

Breath awakens balance.

Silence awakens wisdom.

Together, they help the child blossom from within.

When a classroom learns to breathe, to pause, to observe, and to be still, learning transforms.

The mind becomes clearer.

The heart becomes lighter.

The soul becomes awake.

And in that awakening, true education begins.

Section IV

Curriculum as a Living Experience

Chapter 16

Designing Purposeful Curriculum

A meaningful curriculum integrates:

- Academic learning
- Life skills
- Values
- Emotional intelligence
- Creativity
- Local culture

Curriculum should feel alive, not mechanical.

CHAPTER 16

DESIGNING PURPOSEFUL CURRICULUM: MAKING LEARNING A LIVING EXPERIENCE

A curriculum is often mistaken for a stack of textbooks, a timetable, or a checklist of chapters to be completed within a year. But a true curriculum is something far deeper. It is the heartbeat of the educational journey. It shapes the child's thinking, influences their worldview, nurtures their values, and silently constructs the foundation upon which their future identity will stand. When designed with intention, a curriculum becomes a living experience—not a sequence of lessons, but a pathway of growth.

Children do not remember every chapter they study. They remember how certain lessons made them feel, how certain concepts opened their imagination, how certain discussions transformed the way they saw the world, and how certain activities awakened parts of themselves they didn't know existed. A purposeful curriculum is one that honours this emotional truth. It does not aim to fill the mind; it aims to awaken it.

Designing such a curriculum begins with understanding the child. A curriculum must serve the learner, not the other way around. Children learn best when what they learn feels meaningful, relevant, and connected to life. When learning becomes an isolated academic task, detached from the child's reality, it loses both its sweetness and its purpose. But when learning reflects life—the environment, culture, emotions, society, nature, and human experiences—it becomes alive.

A purposeful curriculum therefore integrates both knowledge and wisdom. Knowledge teaches the child how the world works. Wisdom teaches them how *they* can work in the world. Knowledge trains the mind. Wisdom nurtures the heart. A curriculum that offers only knowledge creates capable workers. A curriculum that offers wisdom creates compassionate human beings.

Such a curriculum grows from a clear intention. What kind of world do we hope to prepare children for? What kind of individuals do we hope they become? These questions lie at the core of purposeful design. Education should not merely prepare children to pass exams; it should prepare them to live with dignity, awareness, empathy, and responsibility.

When designing curriculum, it is important to create a balance—between structure and creativity, between academic demands and emotional nourishment, between discipline and freedom, between tradition and innovation. Children need consistency but also space to explore. They need foundational skills but also opportunities for imagination. Purposeful curriculum honours both sides of learning: the logical and the intuitive, the scientific and the artistic, the measurable and the intangible.

A meaningful curriculum weaves subjects into each other. Mathematics is not taught in isolation but linked to patterns in nature, budgeting in life, architecture in culture. Science is not confined to textbooks but connected to real-world phenomena, environmental issues, and hands-on exploration. Social science is used to ignite empathy, cultural understanding, and a sense of social responsibility. Languages are taught not merely as grammar and vocabulary but as tools of expression, creativity, and identity.

An intentional curriculum also brings local culture into the classroom. It celebrates regional stories, festivals, crafts, traditions, soils, flora, fauna, and community practices. This helps children appreciate their roots, develop cultural pride, and build a grounded sense of belonging. In a world rapidly becoming global, grounding children in their local identities gives them emotional stability and self-worth.

Another crucial aspect of curriculum design is values. Values are not taught through moral science chapters alone; they are infused quietly into learning experiences. A curriculum that includes collaboration teaches respect. One that encourages reflection teaches mindfulness. One that integrates service teaches compassion. One that promotes questioning teaches courage. Values weave themselves into the child's character through the experiences the curriculum creates.

A purposeful curriculum also respects the natural stages of child development. Young children need stories, play, movement, sensory exploration, and emotional bonding. Older children need reasoning, creativity, experimentation, dialogue, and application. Adolescents need identity formation, emotional literacy, life skills, future planning, and ethical grounding. When curriculum aligns with developmental needs, learning becomes not only smoother but more joyful.

A living curriculum also recognises that children learn at different paces. It offers options, flexibility, and multiple pathways to understanding. It encourages project-based learning, portfolios, group work, reflective journals, outdoor learning, and creative expression. These approaches allow children to demonstrate understanding in ways that resonate with their personality, rather than conforming to one rigid model.

Technology may support curriculum, but it should never replace the human touch. Purposeful curriculum uses technology as a tool, not as a teacher. The warmth of human connection, the nuance of classroom discussion, the empathy in a teacher's voice—these are elements no digital platform can replicate.

Assessment, too, becomes meaningful when aligned with purposeful curriculum. Instead of testing memory alone, assessments can evaluate understanding, creativity, collaboration, reflection, problem-solving, and communication. When assessment becomes humane, children no longer fear it; they see it as part of their growth.

A purposeful curriculum is not static. It evolves with society, with the classroom, with the child's needs, and with the teacher's insights. It grows like a living organism—flexible, adaptive, responsive. A teacher becomes both a gardener and a guide, nurturing growth while allowing freedom.

Ultimately, a purposeful curriculum does not aim to produce standardised outcomes. It aims to produce awakened individuals. Children who can think for themselves, express themselves, question respectfully, choose wisely, care deeply, and live consciously.

A curriculum designed with intention becomes a gift—a gift that children carry into adulthood, long after textbooks fade. It becomes the inner compass that guides their decisions, relationships, goals, identity, and purpose.

Education becomes meaningful only when curriculum becomes humane.

And curriculum becomes humane only when it honours the child as a whole —

mind, heart, body, and soul.

Here is your **FULLY ELABORATED, CULTURALLY RICH, PUBLISH-READY CHAPTER 17**, written with emotional warmth, heritage depth, and a smooth literary flow—exactly like a high-quality educational book chapter.

Chapter 17

Culture & Heritage in Teaching

Teaching rooted in culture creates pride and belonging.

Include:

- Folk stories
- Local crafts
- Regional literature
- Festivals
- Traditional wisdom

Children who know their roots grow with confidence.

CHAPTER 17

CULTURE, HERITAGE & LOCAL KNOWLEDGE: ROOTING EDUCATION IN IDENTITY

Every child carries an unseen inheritance. It rests not in their hands, but in their stories, memories, traditions, language, soil, and the rhythm of the place they call home. This inheritance is the cultural heartbeat that shapes their identity long before they enter a classroom. Yet, modern education often treats this inheritance as irrelevant, focusing instead on global ideas, abstract knowledge, and standardized curriculum that may overlook the child's lived reality.

A truly meaningful education recognises that a child does not walk into school empty. They arrive carrying centuries of wisdom, embedded in the songs their grandparents sang, in the stories their parents told them, in the festivals they celebrated, in the food they eat, the crafts they see, the nature around them, and the values their community breathes. When teachers acknowledge this heritage, they water the roots of the child. When they ignore it, the child feels disconnected—from learning, from identity, and eventually from themselves.

Culture is not merely tradition; it is lived experience. It is the way of thinking, feeling, celebrating, grieving, communicating, and belonging. When culture enters the classroom, learning gains a soul. Knowledge becomes meaningful. Lessons become relatable. Children begin to see themselves in what they learn, and suddenly education stops feeling foreign—it becomes personal.

A curriculum that integrates culture and heritage transforms simple topics into alive, meaningful experiences. A geography lesson becomes richer when connected to local rivers, hills, and climate. A science lesson becomes engaging when linked to traditional practices like rainwater harvesting, herbal medicine, or farming cycles. A language lesson becomes beautiful when infused with folk songs, regional stories, and community idioms. A history lesson becomes emotional when children learn about the heroes, freedom fighters, artisans, poets, and leaders of their own soil.

When children see their culture represented in learning material, their confidence blossoms. They feel that their lives matter, their families matter, their traditions matter. It is a subtle but powerful validation—a child realises, "Education is not separate from who I am. It includes me." This inclusion heals the silent distance many children feel between their home world and the world of school.

Local knowledge is an untapped treasure in education. Every community, every region holds unique wisdom—knowledge of soils, seasons, medicinal plants, crafts, architecture, climate, farming practices, music, stories, and survival techniques. This knowledge is not primitive; it is profound. It carries centuries of trial, observation, adaptation, and lived understanding. When teachers bring local knowledge into the classroom, they honour the intelligence of generations.

Imagine a teacher discussing environmental conservation using local case studies—a nearby lake that was restored by villagers, a traditional irrigation method, or a community tree-planting ritual. Suddenly, environmental science feels real.

Children understand that sustainability is not just a global concern; it is a responsibility rooted in their own community.

Culture and heritage also make learning emotional. Children feel pride when they learn about the greatness of their region, the artistry of local craftsmen, or the resilience of their ancestors. A story about a local hero can inspire more courage than chapters filled with distant facts. When children feel pride, they develop a stronger identity. A strong identity fosters confidence, moral grounding, and a sense of belonging.

In multicultural classrooms, cultural sharing becomes a bridge of empathy. Children learn to appreciate differences instead of fearing them. They understand that every culture has beauty, wisdom, and history. Such classrooms become vibrant spaces where languages mix freely, traditions coexist harmoniously, and children grow into citizens who respect diversity.

However, integrating culture does not mean excluding modernity. It means harmonising the two. A balanced education encourages children to embrace the global world while staying rooted in their own heritage. It teaches them to speak English fluently but also honour their mother tongue. It prepares them for modern careers but also makes them aware of their cultural responsibilities. A child who knows where they come from walks into the world with greater confidence, stability, and self-respect.

Teachers play a profound role in this process. When a teacher shares folk tales with expression, children absorb values without feeling lectured. When they invite local artisans into the classroom, learning becomes experiential. When they incorporate regional festivals into activities, children understand the meaning behind rituals. When they say, "Let's write a poem in your mother tongue," or "Tell us about a tradition from your home," children feel emotionally included.

Such gestures are not small. They are transformational. They tell the child, "Your identity matters. Your culture matters. You matter."

In a time when globalisation is rapidly homogenising childhoods, bringing culture into education becomes even more important. Without cultural grounding, children may grow intellectually but feel emotionally rootless. They may know how to use technology but not know who they are. Heritage provides this anchoring—a sense of continuity, connection, and community.

Culture also nurtures values effortlessly. Respect, gratitude, humility, resilience, creativity, devotion—these values live within stories, rituals, folk songs, traditions, and local practices. They do not need to be taught through force; they get absorbed through experience.

Education that honours culture becomes education that honours humanity. It respects the richness of every child's background. It bridges home and school. It strengthens identity. It fosters empathy. It nurtures creativity. And it offers children something far greater than academic success—it offers them belonging.

A child rooted in their culture grows with wings that fly confidently into the world.

A child connected to their heritage becomes a grounded, compassionate adult.

A child whose curriculum reflects their identity develops a lifelong love for learning.

Culture is not a chapter in a textbook.

It is the heartbeat of education.

When we teach through culture, we do not just inform —

we awaken pride, connection, and meaning.

Chapter 18

Nep 2020 & Soulful Pedagogy

NEP 2020 emphasizes:

- Holistic learning
- Multilingualism
- Experiential classrooms
- Art integration
- Flexibility
- Life skills

Soulful pedagogy is the heart behind NEP's structure.

CHAPTER 18

INTEGRATING NEP 2020 WITH SOULFUL PEDAGOGY: BRIDGING POLICY AND HEART

Educational policies are often documents filled with guidelines, objectives, and frameworks. They describe what must be taught, how learning should be assessed, and what structures should be in place. Yet, a policy—no matter how visionary—cannot transform education on its own. Its real power emerges only when it meets the heart of the teacher. When policy meets pedagogy infused with humanity, something extraordinary happens. That is the bridge NEP 2020 invites teachers to build.

The National Education Policy 2020 is not merely a reform document. It is a philosophical shift—a return to holistic, child-centred, culturally grounded education that India's ancient learning systems once embodied. But reading the policy and implementing it are two very different realities. The bridge between the two is the soul of the teacher. When teachers integrate NEP 2020 with soulful pedagogy, the policy comes alive—not on paper, but in the hearts and experiences of children.

NEP 2020 emphasises joyful learning, flexibility, creativity, inclusivity, and holistic development. These concepts are not new; they have always been present in India's educational heritage. What is new is the attempt to embed them into modern schooling systemically. To truly integrate NEP 2020, teachers must go beyond compliance and engage with the essence of the policy—its intention to honour the child's natural rhythms of learning

One of the most profound alignments between NEP 2020 and soulful pedagogy is the focus on *holistic development*. NEP clearly states that education must nurture cognitive, emotional, social, ethical, and physical growth. Soulful pedagogy naturally recognises that children are not brains alone; they are hearts, bodies, imaginations, and spirits. A teacher who teaches with awareness ensures that every lesson touches not just the intellect but the inner being of the child.

Another core element of NEP is *experiential learning*. This is the heart of soulful pedagogy. When children learn by doing, by observing, by interacting, by exploring, and by reflecting, they do not merely memorise information—they internalise it. Experiential learning transforms the classroom into a vibrant space of discovery. It respects the child's innate curiosity and allows learning to unfold organically. NEP encourages schools to replace rote learning with real-world engagement. A soulful teacher does this effortlessly because they know that knowledge gained through experience becomes wisdom.

NEP 2020 also celebrates *multilingualism* and the use of the mother tongue as a foundational learning medium. Soulful pedagogy sees language as more than communication; it is identity, belonging, memory, and emotional safety. A child learning in their mother tongue feels seen. They learn faster, express better, and think more clearly. The shift towards linguistic inclusivity is a shift towards emotional inclusivity. When teachers respect a child's language, they honour the child's soul.

One of the most revolutionary aspects of NEP is its emphasis on *flexible pathways* and *reduced academic pressure*. It acknowledges that children have different speeds, interests, intelligences, and ways of understanding the world. Soulful pedagogy aligns perfectly with this vision. A soulful teacher does not measure all children with the same scale. They adapt methods, differentiate instruction, and create space for every child's unique way of learning. Flexibility is not a disruption; it is compassion in action.

NEP's call for *competency-based assessments* also finds a natural place in soulful teaching. Traditional testing measures memory; competency-based assessment measures understanding. It values growth over performance, effort over perfection, and learning over marks. A soulful teacher sees assessment as an opportunity for reflection, not judgment. When assessment becomes humane, children no longer fear failure—they see it as part of learning.

Another powerful alignment is NEP's emphasis on *well-being*—mental, emotional, and physical. Soulful pedagogy has always prioritised well-being. It understands that a stressed child cannot learn, an anxious child cannot focus, and an emotionally burdened child cannot absorb. By integrating practices like mindfulness, storytelling, play, connection, and open dialogues, the teacher creates a classroom climate where children feel safe, valued, and supported.

NEP's focus on *integrating arts, sports, and vocational skills* also resonates deeply with soulful teaching. These fields nurture creativity, confidence, collaboration, and real-world skills—qualities that build character and resilience. Soulful teachers understand that learning does not happen only through books; it happens through music, movement, craft, curiosity, and the expressions of the human spirit.

The shift towards *inclusive education*, highlighted strongly in NEP, is perhaps one of the most heart-aligned elements of the policy. Inclusion is not only about providing accommodations for children with special needs; it is about accepting and honouring diversity. Soulful pedagogy already embraces this truth. It sees each child as a unique light and ensures that no child feels left out or unseen. Inclusivity is not a strategy; it is a mindset, one that treats differences as strengths rather than shortcomings.

To integrate NEP 2020 meaningfully, teachers must create classrooms that reflect the policy's spirit—not just its structure. This means creating lessons that invite curiosity, building relationships that inspire trust, designing activities that awaken imagination, giving children choices that build autonomy, and seeing each learner as a whole person rather than a number on a report card.

Teachers become the bridge-bearers of NEP. Policies can outline objectives, but only teachers can breathe life into them. Implementation does not require perfection; it requires intention. A small shift—a moment of mindful listening, a simple real-life connection to a lesson, a flexible activity, a kind word, a creative learning task—can echo the spirit of NEP in powerful ways.

The heart of NEP 2020 is a return to humanity in education.

The heart of soulful pedagogy is the same.

When these two hearts meet, education becomes transformative.

A teacher who blends NEP with soulful teaching does not simply follow a policy—they create a movement. A movement where learning becomes joyful, where classrooms become compassionate, where children grow with confidence, and where education becomes an experience that nourishes the mind, heart, and spirit.

This is the education India dreams of—and it begins in the hands and hearts of teachers who teach with soul.

Chapter 19

Assessment for Growth, Not Fear

Assessment should measure:

- Progress
- Effort
- Understanding
- Reflection
- Not just marks.

Assessment must help children grow, not shrink.

CHAPTER 19

ASSESSMENT FOR GROWTH, NOT FEAR: REDEFINING HOW WE MEASURE LEARNING

Assessment is one of the most misunderstood elements of education. For decades, it has been used as a tool to judge children, rank them, compare them, or place them into categories of "good," "average," or "weak." The purpose of assessment gradually shifted from understanding the child to evaluating their mistakes; from nurturing learning to monitoring performance; from guiding growth to creating pressure. In this shift something deeply valuable was lost—the child's joy, curiosity, confidence, and inner motivation.

Assessment, at its heart, was never meant to frighten children. It was meant to illuminate learning. It was designed to help teachers see where a child needs support, where they shine, what they understand, and how they think. Assessment is a mirror for the teacher, not a label for the child. But when this mirror becomes a weapon, children begin to fear learning itself.

The tragedy of fear-based assessment is silent but profound. A child who fears mistakes stops taking risks. A child who fears marks stops exploring new ideas. A child who fears judgment stops asking questions. And a child who fears exams learns not to understand but to memorise. Slowly, learning becomes a burden, and the natural spark that every child carries begins to dim.

To create an education system where every child flourishes, we must shift from *assessment of learning* to *assessment for learning*. This shift changes everything—the purpose, the process, the emotions, and the outcomes.

Assessment for growth begins with understanding that learning is not a straight line. It is a process of exploration, confusion, understanding, forgetting, rediscovering, and finally internalising. A child who struggles today may bloom tomorrow. A child who learns slowly may understand more deeply. A child who makes mistakes may develop more resilience than one who always gets everything right. Growth cannot be measured in weekly tests; it can only be seen through patient observation and compassionate guidance.

When assessment becomes growth-oriented, the teacher becomes a guide rather than a judge. They observe without shaming, correct without humiliating, and support without comparing. In such a classroom, children do not fear mistakes—they learn from them. They do not hide their doubts—they express them. They do not pretend to understand—they seek clarity. The energy of assessment transforms from anxiety to curiosity.

In a growth-based system, feedback becomes the heart of assessment. But feedback is not a red mark on a notebook or a number circled at the top of the page. True feedback speaks to the child as a human being. It says, "I see your effort," "I notice your progress," "Here is something we can work on together," "You can improve, and I believe you will." Feedback becomes a conversation, not a verdict. It nurtures confidence rather than damaging it.

One of the most powerful aspects of growth-based assessment is that it teaches children self-reflection. Instead of always looking outward for evaluation, they begin to look inward. They ask themselves:

What did I do well today?

Where did I struggle?

What can I try differently next time?

These questions build resilience, metacognition, and emotional maturity. The child begins to understand that learning is not an event but a journey—and that every journey has moments of struggle and moments of triumph.

Assessment for growth also respects the diversity of learning styles. Not every child can express their understanding through written tests. Some understand better through speaking, others through drawing, others through hands-on projects, and others through practical application. When assessment becomes flexible, children finally get the opportunity to show their true abilities. The quiet child who writes beautifully, the expressive child who explains concepts aloud, the artistic child who creates visual models—all find their space to shine.

Moreover, assessment for growth depends on observation—subtle, continuous, sensitive observation. A teacher who watches the child's behaviour, interest, curiosity, teamwork, effort, and attitude gains a far deeper understanding than any test score can provide. A single number cannot capture a child's intelligence, character, creativity, or emotional depth. But a teacher's understanding can.

A humane assessment system also considers the emotional state of the learner. A child who is anxious, unwell, grieving, or distracted cannot perform at their best. Growth-oriented teachers recognise this humanity. They extend compassion instead of pressure. They know that every child has days of difficulty. They measure learning over time, not in a single moment.

In such a classroom, assessment becomes a shared responsibility. The teacher reflects, the student reflects, and both work together to support learning. This builds a relationship of trust—the foundation of all meaningful education.

When assessment shifts from fear to growth, children rediscover the joy of learning. They become active participants rather than passive receivers. They take ownership rather than feeling controlled. They begin to see mistakes as opportunities rather than failures. Their confidence blossoms. Their curiosity deepens. Their love for learning returns.

The teacher, too, undergoes transformation. They move from monitoring to mentoring, from policing to guiding, from correcting to nurturing. Teaching becomes less about performance and more about partnership.

In the wider picture, growth-based assessment creates a society of resilient, reflective, and emotionally balanced individuals—people who understand that excellence is not measured by scores alone but by effort, adaptability, and integrity.

When assessment becomes humane, education becomes humane.

When assessment supports growth, learning becomes joyful.

And when assessment empowers children, it shapes a future grounded in confidence rather than fear.

The purpose of assessment is not to label the child.

It is to illuminate their path.

Not to measure their limits, but to expand their possibilities.

Not to judge who they are, but to guide who they can become.

Chapter 20

Creating Holistic Learning Environments

A classroom should feel like a place where:

- Children feel safe
- Ideas flow
- Mistakes are welcomed
- Creativity blossoms

Learning is not a session—it is a climate.

CHAPTER 20

CREATING HOLISTIC LEARNING ENVIRONMENTS: SPACES THAT NURTURE THE CHILD

A classroom is not merely a room. It is a universe.

Children do not step into it as blank slates—they arrive carrying emotions, curiosities, worries, dreams, energy, fatigue, excitement, hesitation, and unspoken stories. A classroom that acknowledges these inner realities becomes a sanctuary. A classroom that ignores them becomes a pressure chamber. The difference lies in how consciously the learning environment is crafted.

A holistic learning environment recognises that education is not an academic transaction. It is an emotional, physical, mental, and spiritual journey where the child needs nurturing at every layer of their being. Such environments do not emerge by accident. They are created purposefully, with sensitivity and awareness—shaped by the teacher's mindset, behaviour, compassion, and the energy they bring into the space.

The first element of a holistic environment is emotional safety. A child needs to feel safe before they can learn. When the classroom becomes a place where mistakes are not punished, where fears are heard, where questions are welcomed, and where every child feels valued, the mind relaxes. Only in this relaxed state can true learning occur. A child who fears embarrassment or judgment learns with a closed mind. A child who feels emotionally safe learns with an open heart.

Emotional safety is created not through rules but through relationships. A teacher who greets children warmly, listens with full attention, uses gentle tone, and responds with empathy creates an emotional climate where students feel seen. The smallest gestures—a reassuring smile, a quiet moment of connection, the acknowledgement of effort—become invisible pillars of emotional wellbeing.

Holistic learning environments also honour the body. Traditional classrooms often expect children to sit still for long periods, ignoring their natural need for movement. But a child's body is a living part of their learning. Movement stimulates the brain, increases focus, reduces stress, and awakens curiosity. A holistic classroom allows children to stretch, walk, breathe, participate, and engage physically—not as a break from learning, but as part of learning itself. A child who feels physically free can explore mentally without restriction.

The physical environment also plays a silent yet powerful role. A classroom does not need expensive decor to be nurturing. It needs warmth. Natural light, thoughtful seating, greenery, clean spaces, displays of children's work, and a peaceful arrangement of materials create an atmosphere that invites calmness and focus. When the classroom feels like a living space rather than a rigid institution, children feel at home in their learning journey.

In holistic environments, the mind is not overloaded—it is gently guided. Instead of rushing through chapters, teachers weave learning with curiosity, storytelling, reflection, and hands-on activities. Lessons are not delivered mechanically; they unfold organically. The teacher becomes a facilitator of experiences rather than a dispenser of information. Here, the mind grows because it is nourished—not pressured.

Another essential aspect of holistic environments is the nurturing of relationships—not just between teacher and child, but among peers. Many children come to school carrying loneliness. A classroom that fosters collaboration, kindness, teamwork, and empathy becomes a community rather than a collection of individuals. These social bonds give children emotional courage. They learn to support each other, celebrate each other, and accept differences with grace.

Spiritual nourishment also plays a subtle yet profound role. Spirituality here does not refer to religion, but to the nourishment of the child's inner self. Moments of silence, breathing practices, gratitude reflections, nature walks, art expression, and mindful pauses help children look inward. In these moments, children reconnect with their emotions, find their calmness, and strengthen their sense of self. A holistic classroom teaches children not only how to succeed, but how to be grounded.

Creativity is another heartbeat of holistic learning. Children flourish when they are allowed to imagine, paint, build, write, explore, innovate, question, and create. A classroom that encourages creativity is a classroom that respects individuality. When creativity flows, confidence grows. The child feels, "My ideas matter." This sense of worth becomes a lifelong asset.

Holistic environments also respect diversity. Every child brings a unique personality, learning pace, emotional world, cultural background, and set of strengths. A classroom that embraces this diversity makes every child feel included. Differences become sources of learning rather than barriers. Inclusion is not a policy—it is an attitude.

One of the most powerful elements of a holistic environment is the teacher's presence. A mindful teacher transforms the atmosphere simply by the way they stand, speak, listen, and respond. Their calmness becomes contagious. Their compassion becomes a healing force. Their authenticity creates trust. In such a space, discipline becomes natural, not forced—because children respect the person who respects them.

Holistic environments do not eliminate challenges; they transform how children meet those challenges. A child who feels emotionally strong, physically free, mentally stimulated, creatively expressive, spiritually grounded, and socially connected becomes resilient. Such a child does not fear learning. They do not fear failure. They do not fear the world. They walk with a sense of inner security that carries them far beyond the classroom.

In the end, a holistic learning environment does not teach only subjects. It teaches life. It gives children the tools to understand themselves, to navigate emotions, to collaborate with others, to think deeply, to stay curious, and to grow with integrity. These are the skills that shape not just academic success but human success.

A classroom built with holistic intention becomes a sanctuary of growth —a place where the child's mind expands, their heart opens, their spirit steadies, and their potential unfolds naturally.

This is the kind of environment every child deserves. And it begins with the vision, sensitivity, and love of the teacher who creates it.

Section V

The Guru as a Leader

Chapter 21

The Teacher as Leader

A teacher leads not through authority, but through authenticity.

Leadership qualities:

- Clarity
- Courage
- Integrity
- Kindness
- Consistency

A teacher is the emotional leader of the class.

CHAPTER 21

TEACHER–PARENT PARTNERSHIPS: BUILDING A CIRCLE OF TRUST AROUND THE CHILD

A child's world is shaped by two powerful forces—home and school.

At home, the child receives love, belonging, identity, and the earliest lessons of life.

At school, the child receives knowledge, social understanding, skills, and exposure to the wider world.

When these two forces work in harmony, the child grows with confidence and emotional security.

But when they move in opposite directions, the child becomes confused, anxious, and vulnerable.

A powerful truth in education is this:

A child develops best when the adults around them form a circle of trust.

This circle is formed when teachers and parents work together—not as separate authorities, but as partners walking towards the same goal: the well-being of the child.

Yet, through decades, the teacher–parent relationship has often been strained or distant. Schools sometimes expect parents to stay silent. Parents sometimes expect teachers to handle everything. Miscommunication, unrealistic expectations, and emotional gaps lead to misunderstandings that affect the child most deeply. Behind every behavioural issue, every emotional dip, every academic struggle, there is often a lack of alignment between home and school.

A meaningful teacher–parent partnership begins with simple awareness:

Both sides love the child. Both want the child to succeed. Both see different parts of the child's world.

Parents see the child's emotions, vulnerabilities, habits, and family realities.

Teachers see the child's learning patterns, social behaviour, strengths, and classroom confidence.

When these perspectives meet, a fuller, richer, more accurate understanding of the child emerges.

The foundation of this partnership is communication—genuine, warm, honest communication that focuses on the child rather than blame. When teachers communicate not only problems but also progress, when they speak with respect rather than authority, when they listen rather than instruct, trust begins to bloom. Parents feel valued, not judged. Teachers feel supported, not criticised. And the child feels surrounded by understanding adults.

Communication should be frequent, not only during report card days. Small updates, encouraging messages, brief conversations, and periodic sharing of observations create a bridge that strengthens slowly but powerfully. A parent who feels informed becomes a parent who is supportive. A teacher who feels heard becomes a teacher who is empowered.

Partnership also requires empathy. Parents carry stresses of their own—work pressures, financial responsibilities, personal challenges, or emotional fatigue. Teachers, too, carry heavy loads—multiple children, administrative tasks, deadlines, and emotional labour. When both sides approach each other with empathy rather than expectations, the relationship softens. Instead of "Why didn't you do this?" the tone shifts to "How can we support each other to help the child?"

In such moments, partnership becomes real.

Understanding boundaries is another essential part of this relationship. Parents should trust the teacher's professional insight, and teachers should respect the parent's intimate knowledge of the child's life. When boundaries are respected, neither side feels controlled or undermined. Instead, they meet as equals in a shared mission.

A healthy teacher–parent partnership also recognises that children behave differently in different environments. A quiet child at home may be active in school. A cheerful child in class may be withdrawn at home. A child who listens easily at home may struggle with peer influence at school. These differences are normal. When teachers and parents share observations without judgment, they begin to understand the child holistically rather than through isolated incidents.

Many behavioural and academic concerns can be resolved simply through alignment. When parents reinforce classroom values at home—punctuality, respect, effort, curiosity—children feel consistency. When teachers consider the family's cultural, emotional, or financial realities, the child feels supported rather than pressured. This alignment gives the child stability—an inner anchor that guides them in moments of confusion.

Celebration of the child is another key component. When both home and school acknowledge the child's efforts, talents, uniqueness, and strengths, the child's self-esteem blossoms. A child who feels celebrated at both ends of their world develops confidence, resilience, and a strong identity. They feel safe to take risks, explore new ideas, and believe in themselves.

Partnership also includes being united in handling challenges. When a child misbehaves, struggles academically, or shows emotional changes, teachers and parents should come together gently, not reactively. Instead of blame, they should bring curiosity. Instead of punishment, they should bring understanding. Children sense unity. They sense division too. When adults stand together, the child feels protected and guided rather than threatened.

The teacher–parent partnership becomes extremely powerful when it evolves beyond formality into genuine connection. When teachers know the names of family members, when parents know the teacher's efforts, when both express gratitude for each other, the partnership becomes emotional rather than transactional. This emotional bond forms a protective circle around the child—a circle filled with safety, trust, and care.

In this circle, the child thrives.

They know that if they fall, someone will catch them.

If they struggle, someone will guide them.

If they dream, someone will support them.

If they grow, someone will celebrate them.

A child surrounded by such adults walks into the world with courage.

In this partnership, the teacher becomes an extended family members and the parent becomes an extended educator. Together they do not shape just academic success—they shape the child's character, values, emotional stability, and identity.

A powerful future always grows from a strong circle of trust.

When teachers and parents walk hand in hand, the child does not walk alone—they walk with a village behind them.

Chapter 22

Communication, Conflict & Harmony

Healthy communication builds a positive classroom culture.

Conflict is not failure—it is an opportunity to teach:

- Respect
- Negotiation
- Empathy
- Understanding

Harmony grows when communication is conscious.

CHAPTER 22

THE EMOTIONALLY AWARE TEACHER: THE HEART THAT GUIDES THE CLASSROOM

A teacher's presence is more powerful than their lesson plan.

A teacher's tone teaches as much as their words.

A teacher's emotional state shapes the emotional climate of the entire classroom.

This is why emotional awareness is not an optional skill for teachers—it is a foundational quality. A teacher who understands emotions, both their own and those of children, becomes a lighthouse in the classroom. Their presence offers direction, safety, and steadiness even when the waves of daily challenges rise high.

Children learn emotional cues from the adults around them. A teacher who remains calm while handling misbehaviour teaches self-regulation. A teacher who listens with patience teaches empathy. A teacher who apologizes when wrong teaches humility. A teacher who expresses joy authentically teaches emotional openness. In this way, emotional awareness becomes a silent curriculum—more powerful than any textbook chapter.

Being an emotionally aware teacher begins with self-awareness.

How do I feel today?

What energy am I bringing into the classroom?

What emotions are shaping my words, my reactions, my decisions?

A teacher who pauses to ask these questions prevents emotional overflow. They do not project personal stress onto children. They do not react impulsively. They do not allow irritation to become their mode of communication. Instead, they use awareness as a filter, ensuring that what reaches the child is compassion, clarity, and guidance.

Emotional awareness also means understanding that children's behaviour is a language. When a child is restless, they may be anxious. When they are withdrawn, they may be overwhelmed. When they are loud, they may be seeking connection. When they refuse to work, they may be feeling inadequate. Emotionally aware teachers look beyond behaviour and search for the feeling beneath it. They respond not to the symptom but to the root.

This sensitivity transforms the classroom. Instead of blame, the teacher brings curiosity. Instead of anger, they bring patience. Instead of punishment, they bring understanding. In such an environment, children feel emotionally safe—and safety is the soil in which learning grows.

Emotional awareness also means managing one's own responses wisely. Teaching can be emotionally exhausting. There are days when the class feels chaotic, when responsibilities weigh heavily, when personal problems enter the mind, or when children push boundaries. An emotionally aware teacher does not deny these challenges—they acknowledge them. But they also know how to separate their inner world from their professional role. They practise calmness, grounding, mindful breathing or small moments of pause to reset their emotional energy. This emotional discipline becomes a gift the teacher gives to themselves and their students.

A teacher who is emotionally aware also becomes a model for authentic expression. They show children that emotions are not weaknesses, but natural experiences. They teach children to express respectfully, to reflect on feelings, to communicate openly. When a teacher says, "I understand you're upset, let's talk about it," the child learns emotional literacy. When the teacher says, "I'm feeling tired today, but I'm here," the child learns honesty without burden. When the teacher says, "Let's take a moment to breathe," the child learns regulation.

Emotional awareness strengthens relationships in the classroom. Children trust teachers who understand them. They open up more. They share their fears, confusions, and joys. They feel seen. They feel valued. They feel understood. And this connection becomes the foundation upon which strong learning is built.

An emotionally aware teacher also recognises their own limits. They know when to seek support, when to rest, and when to step back momentarily to restore inner balance. They break free from the myth that teachers must be perfect. Instead, they choose authenticity—which is far more powerful. Children do not need perfect teachers. They need present teachers. Teachers who feel deeply, reflect consciously, and respond wisely.

Emotional awareness develops empathy—the ability to feel with another. Empathy softens discipline and strengthens boundaries. It makes the teacher firm without being harsh, corrective without being hurtful, guiding without being controlling. When children sense empathy, their behaviour naturally softens. They cooperate not out of fear, but out of respect.

This is the true essence of emotional leadership—the ability to influence children's behaviour through emotional intelligence rather than authority. An emotionally aware teacher leads with heart, not with control. They create harmony rather than tension. Their presence brings stability, clarity, and safety to the classroom.

Emotional awareness also expands the teacher's understanding of diversity. Not every child expresses emotions in the same way. Some cry easily, others hide their fears. Some ask questions loudly, others silently struggle. Some seek attention, others seek invisibility. An emotionally aware teacher respects these differences. They do not force children into one mold. They allow each child's emotional personality to unfold naturally.

With emotional awareness, even the teacher's voice becomes a tool of transformation. A gentle voice can de-escalate conflict. A steady voice can calm anxiety. A warm voice can inspire effort. A reflective voice can invite introspection. Children learn to regulate their emotions through the tone of the adults around them.

When emotional awareness becomes part of teaching, the classroom no longer feels like a battlefield of rules and discipline. It becomes a space of understanding, relationship, and growth. Children learn not only academics but emotional skills—skills that will guide them throughout life. They learn empathy, resilience, patience, self-regulation, communication, and compassion.

And the teacher? They evolve too. They grow emotionally stronger, more peaceful, more grounded. They find deeper meaning in their work. They experience less burnout because they understand their emotions instead of suppressing them. They build deeper connections with students, making teaching not just a job but a profound human experience.

In the end, the emotionally aware teacher is not defined by how well they control the class but by how well they connect with it.

Not by how much they teach, but by how deeply they touch.

Not by the content they deliver, but by the calmness, empathy, and awareness they bring into every moment.

The emotionally aware teacher is the heart of the classroom.

A steady light in the child's life.

A guide not just of knowledge, but of emotional wisdom.

Someone the child remembers long after textbooks fade.

Chapter 23

Teacher Wellness

A tired teacher cannot inspire.

A stressed mind cannot create joy.

Teacher wellness includes:

- Emotional boundaries
- Daily relaxation
- Self-reflection
- Support systems
- Work–life balance

Nurture yourself to nurture others.

CHAPTER 23

HEALING THROUGH EDUCATION: THE CLASSROOM AS A PLACE OF TRANSFORMATION

Every child who walks into a classroom carries an invisible story.

Some carry joy.

Some carry fear.

Some carry silence.

Some carry wounds so deep that even they cannot name them.

Some carry burdens that do not belong to their age.

In the modern world, children encounter emotional challenges that earlier generations could not have imagined—fast-changing family structures, academic pressure, overstimulation, loneliness, digital competition, performance anxiety and unspoken trauma. Often, these inner storms remain hidden behind a smile, a restless behaviour, or a seemingly ordinary routine. Beneath the surface, many children are quietly struggling.

This is why education must become more than teaching—it must become healing.

Healing in education does not mean therapy in the clinical sense. It means creating classroom experiences, relationships, and environments that soothe the mind, soften the heart, and strengthen the spirit. When education becomes healing, children do not merely learn—they recover. They regain confidence, rediscover joy, rebuild trust, and return to themselves.

A classroom becomes a healing space when it welcomes the child as they are. Not as how they "should" be, not as how society demands, but as how they arrive—imperfect, confused, curious, sensitive, beautiful in their own rhythms. Healing begins the moment a child feels accepted without judgment. A teacher's presence, tone, and kindness become the first medicine.

Healing begins in the subtle ways a teacher speaks.

A gentle voice can calm anxiety.

A patient response can heal frustration.

A warm "It's okay, try again" can mend fear of failure.

A reassuring smile can soothe loneliness.

A listening ear can heal a thousand unspoken feelings.

Teachers may never fully know how deeply their words affect a child—but children always remember how their teachers made them feel. For some children, school becomes the only place where they feel emotionally safe. For some, a teacher becomes the only adult who believes in them. This belief becomes a lifeline. A child can survive many difficulties when even one adult sees their goodness.

Healing in education also means understanding behaviour as communication. A disruptive child may be seeking stability. A withdrawn child may be protecting themselves. A perfectionist child may be carrying invisible pressure. When teachers approach behaviour with empathy rather than punishment, children experience emotional relief. They feel understood instead of shamed, guided instead of scolded.

The healing classroom also nurtures emotional expression. When children are allowed to talk about their feelings, write their thoughts, draw their fears, role-play their frustrations, or simply sit quietly with their emotions, they learn emotional literacy. They learn that feelings are not dangerous; they are windows into the self. When feelings are acknowledged, they no longer overwhelm.

Another dimension of healing is belonging. A child who feels like an outsider carries deep emotional pain. But when they feel part of a caring community—when classmates greet them, include them, listen to them, and accept their uniqueness—they heal. Belonging repairs emotional isolation. It gives children a sense of place, identity, and security.

Healing also happens through structure and consistency.

A predictable routine calms anxiety.

Clear expectations reduce confusion.

Fair boundaries create safety.

Children thrive when the environment does not suddenly shift beneath their feet.

A steady classroom becomes a psychological anchor.

Nature, too, becomes a healer within education. Time outdoors, exposure to sunlight, connection with plants, soil, wind, and sky restores emotional balance. Nature reminds children that the world is bigger than their worries and gentler than their fears. Even small nature-based activities in the classroom—caring for a plant, watching rain, observing butterflies—can bring peace to an overwhelmed mind.

Creativity is another healing pathway. When children paint, sing, act, dance, write, or build, they channel emotions that may not find words. Creativity opens emotional doors. It allows healing to flow through colour, movement, rhythm, and imagination. Children who create feel empowered. They feel the joy of bringing something new into the world. This joy melts emotional heaviness.

Healing in education does not ignore academic growth—it enhances it. A child whose emotional wounds are acknowledged learns with greater ease. A child who feels safe becomes curious. A child who feels valued participates more. A child whose heart is calm absorbs knowledge like a sponge. Healing strengthens learning because learning requires emotional openness.

A healing teacher is not someone who fixes children's lives. They are someone who walks beside the child with compassion. They do not need psychology degrees. Their power lies in their humanity—the way they speak, listen, hold space, respond, and show warmth. A healing teacher creates a classroom where children feel, "I can be myself here." Sometimes healing comes in a single unforgettable moment—a teacher saying, "I believe in you." a teacher noticing a child's sadness and asking gently, "Are you okay?" a teacher defending a child who feels small or misunderstood.

a teacher celebrating a child who feels invisible.

These moments are seeds planted in the child's memory. They grow into confidence, resilience, and self-worth.

For many children, school becomes the place where they learn that adults can be kind, that mistakes are not sins, and that they are worthy of care. This realisation itself is healing.

When education becomes healing, it transforms not only children but the future. It shapes individuals who grow with empathy, resilience, and emotional intelligence. It creates adults who can handle life's challenges without breaking. It creates citizens who treat others with compassion because compassion was part of their schooling.

In such a world, schools become not institutions but sanctuaries.

Teachers become not instructors but healers.

Learning becomes not pressure but nourishment.

And children become not performers, but whole human beings.

A healing classroom may not change everything in a child's life—but it can change the way the child feels about themselves.

And sometimes, that is enough to change the entire direction of their life.

Here is your **FINAL CHAPTER—FULLY ELABORATED, DEEPLY SPIRITUAL, EMOTIONALLY POWERFUL, AND PUBLISH-READY**, completing your book with grace, meaning, and depth.

This chapter has been written as a beautiful closing reflection—the kind that stays with the reader long after the book ends.

Chapter 24

Walking the Guru Path

The Guru Path is lifelong.

It is a journey of:

- Compassion
- Wisdom
- Courage
- Humility
- Purpose

A guru's legacy is not in textbooks—it is in hearts.

CHAPTER 24

THE TEACHER'S INNER JOURNEY: BECOMING LIGHT FROM WITHIN

Teaching begins in the classroom, but the true journey of a teacher starts within.

Long after lessons fade, long after children graduate, long after textbooks are replaced by new editions, one thing remains—the teacher's inner growth. A teacher's real legacy is not the syllabus they completed but the person they became through the act of teaching.

Every day, teachers enter classrooms carrying their own emotions, struggles, joys, confusions, and hopes. They instruct, guide, nurture, correct, celebrate, comfort, listen, and lead—often without rest and often without acknowledgement. In doing so, they grow in ways they don't always notice. Teaching shapes not only children, but teachers themselves. It chisels the character. It purifies the heart. It awakens the soul.

The inner journey of a teacher begins with self-awareness. Teaching becomes meaningful only when the teacher understands who they are—their strengths, fears, biases, triggers, and values. A teacher who knows themselves teaches with clarity. They do not react blindly. They do not carry unresolved emotions into the classroom. Instead, they become conscious creators of the environment around them.

Self-awareness leads to humility—one of the most beautiful qualities a teacher can possess. Humility allows the teacher to see every child as a teacher too. Every question asked, every behaviour displayed, every moment of conflict, every success, every mistake becomes an opportunity for the teacher to grow. Children reflect our inner world. When teachers recognise this, the classroom becomes not a stage of authority but a space of shared humanity.

The inner journey also involves healing. Teachers carry wounds from their own childhood, from life experiences, from exhaustion, from the emotional weight of their responsibilities. When teachers begin to heal themselves—through reflection, calmness, mindfulness, silence, nature, or support—they teach from a place of emotional abundance rather than emotional depletion. A healed teacher heals others simply through their presence.

Another dimension of this journey is patience. Patience is not about waiting quietly; it is the art of being present without frustration. Children grow in slow, uneven, imperfect ways. They make the same mistakes repeatedly. They resist, they question, they forget, they struggle. A patient teacher understands that growth takes time. They do not give up on children—or on themselves. In patience, teachers discover their greatest strength: endurance with compassion.

The inner journey also awakens wisdom. With each passing year, teachers learn that knowledge alone cannot guide a child. What truly guides is intuition—the soft inner voice shaped by experience, empathy, and awareness. A wise teacher listens to this inner voice. It tells them when to hold a child close, when to step back, when to push, when to pause, when to speak, and when to remain silent. Wisdom makes teaching an art rather than a task.

As teachers grow inwardly, they also discover the power of detachment—not emotional withdrawal, but healthy separation of identity from outcome. They realise that they cannot control everything. They cannot guarantee that every child will excel, behave, listen, or understand immediately. This realisation frees them from unnecessary pressure and allows them to teach with lightness. Detachment helps teachers focus on effort, not results—on sincerity, not perfection.

The inner journey deepens through gratitude. Teachers who practise gratitude find beauty in small moments—a child's smile, a breakthrough in learning, a sincere apology, a silent gesture of respect, a heartfelt "Thank you" from a student. These moments nourish the heart. They remind teachers that their work, though difficult, is sacred. Gratitude transforms teaching from a profession into a prayer.

Reflection becomes another companion on the teacher's inner path. A reflective teacher asks:

"Did I speak kindly today?"

"Did I understand this child well?"

"Could I have responded differently?"

"What did I learn from my students today?"

Reflection does not create guilt—it creates growth. It deepens the teacher's relationship with themselves and with their children.

The inner journey also includes forgiveness—forgiving children, forgiving situations, and above all, forgiving oneself. Teachers often carry guilt for the things they could not change, for the days they lost patience, for the mistakes they made unknowingly. Self-forgiveness releases this weight. It reminds teachers that they, too, are human—learning, evolving, and deserving of compassion.

Teaching is, ultimately, a spiritual path.

Not because it is religious, but because it touches the soul.

A teacher influences not only what a child knows, but who the child becomes.

This responsibility requires teachers to anchor themselves in meaning, purpose, and inner peace.

A teacher on an inner journey becomes a beacon of light. Their presence radiates calmness. Their voice carries stability. Their actions carry thoughtfulness. Their relationships carry authenticity. Children feel this energy. They feel safe. They feel inspired. They feel guided by someone who is not just teaching—but living their own truth.

The inner journey is not a destination. It is a lifelong unfolding. Every child who enters the classroom becomes a chapter in the teacher's growth. Every year becomes a new season of learning. Every experience becomes a step toward deeper understanding.

In the end, teaching is less about shaping the future and more about shaping oneself in the present.

A teacher's inner journey is the quiet heartbeat behind every lesson, every gesture, every moment of connection.

When teachers grow inwardly, education transforms outwardly.

When teachers shine from within, children learn to shine too.

When teachers walk their inner path with honesty and awareness, they become not just educators—but nurturers of humanity.

This is the true completion of the teaching journey.

Not in awards, not in results, not in recognition—but in the silent, profound evolution of the teacher's own soul.

Author Bio

Dr. Shweta Pancholi...as an educator, researcher, and emotional-learning advocate from Gujarat, India. With a strong academic background in English and teacher education, she has dedicated her career to exploring how emotional awareness, cultural sensitivity, and compassionate teaching can transform learning experiences for children—especially those from marginalized communities.

Her work reflects a blend of ancient Indian wisdom, modern emotional psychology, and holistic pedagogy. She writes with clarity and heart, drawing from years of teaching, training, mentoring, and classroom observation. Dr. Pancholi believes that education is not merely an academic process but a healing and humanizing journey. Her voice resonates with teachers, parents, and educators who wish to bring meaning and mindfulness into their practice.

This book is an extension of her vision—**to bring soul back into education, one teacher and one child at a time.**